University of Cincinnati

THE CAMPUS GUIDE

University of Cincinnati

AN ARCHITECTURAL TOUR BY
Paul Bennett

PHOTOGRAPHS BY
Walter Smalling, Jr.

FOREWORD BY
Michael Graves

Princeton Architectural Press
NEW YORK | *2001*

This book has been made possible through the generous support of the Graham Foundation for Advanced Studies in the Fine Arts.

PUBLISHED BY
Princeton Architectural Press
37 East 7th Street
New York, New York 10003

For a free catalog of books, call 1.800.722.6657.
Visit our web site at www.papress.com.

Printed and bound in the United States
04 03 02 01 5 4 3 2 1 First edition

SERIES EDITOR: Jan Cigliano
SERIES CONCEPT: Dennis Looney
DESIGN: Sara E. Stemen
COPYEDITING: Heather Ewing
MAPS: Jane Garvie

SPECIAL THANKS TO: Nettie Aljian, Ann Alter, Amanda Atkins, Nicola Bednarek, Janet Behning, Jane Garvie, Clare Jacobson, Mark Lamster, Nancy Eklund Later, Anne Nitschke, Lottchen Shivers, Jennifer Thompson, and Deb Wood of Princeton Architectural Press —Kevin C. Lippert, publisher

LIBRARY OF CONGRESS CATALOGING-IN-PUBLICATION DATA
Bennett, Paul, 1970–
University of Cincinnati / Paul Bennett : photographs by Walter Smalling, Jr.
p. cm. — (The campus guide)
Includes bibliographical references (p. 123) and index.
ISBN 1-67898-232-1 (alk. paper)
1. University of Cincinnati—Buildings—Guidebooks. 2. University of Cincinnati—Buildings—Pictorial works. I. Smalling, Walter. II. Title. III. Campus guide (New York, N.Y.)
LD984.B46 2001
727'.3'0977178—DC21 00-069218

PRINTED IN CHINA

How to Use this Book

This guide is intended for visitors, alumni, and students who wish to have an insider's look at the most significant and historic buildings on the University of Cincinnati campus, from McMicken, Memorial, and Dyer Halls on the original campus to DAAP and the Sigma Sigma Commons and Campus Green by landscape architect George Hargreaves at the heart of the late twentieth-century campus. Six Walks highlight the most recent signature buildings—including SOM's Edwards Center, Michael Grave's Engineering Research Center, Peter Eisenman's Aronoff Center for Design and Art, Frank Gehry's Vontz Center, Henry Cobb's College-Conservatory of Music, and Leers Winzapfel's Center for Enrollment Services. Each Walk opens with a three-dimensional aerial map that locates the buildings on that walk.

Visitors are welcome to tour the University of Cincinnati campus and its buildings:

Tours Admissions Office. Monday through Saturday; hours vary.
(513) 556-2417

College of Design, Art, Architecture & Planning PO Box 210016.
(513) 556-4933

Langsam Library Monday–Thursday 7:45am to 12 midnight, Friday 7:45am to 9:00pm, Saturday 10:00am to 9:00pm, Sunday 12 noon to midnight.

UC Bookstores

> **West Campus** 123 West University Avenue: Monday–Thursday 8am to 7pm, Friday 8am to 6pm, Saturday 10am to 2pm, Sunday closed; (513) 556-1700.

> **DAAP** 3450 Aronoff Center: Monday–Friday 7:30am to 5:00pm; (513) 556-4672

Main Campus Shuttle (513) 556-2283

Main Campus Parking East Campus: (513) 558-5606
West Campus: (513) 556-2283

Kingsgate Conference Center (513) 487-3800, www.marriott.com

Campus Police (513) 556-4900

Further information
University of Cincinnati
2623 Clifton Avenue
Cincinnati, Ohio 45221-0065
(513) 556-6000
www.uc.edu

Foreword

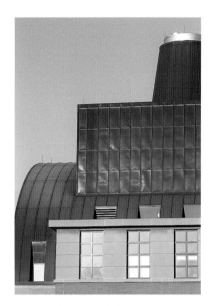

Engineering Research Center

This guide to the University of Cincinnati campus will show you around a very different college than the place I attended in the 1950s. As you tour the campus, try to imagine my friends and I playing Frisbee on the lawn in front of the Sigma Chi House, since demolished, just across the street from the new Engineering Research Center, which I was later selected to design! So I bring you partly a memory piece.

In the 1950s, one was always aware that "UC" was *one* campus with *two* student bodies: one comprised of the residents who lived in fraternity or sorority houses, or dormitories; and the those who came by streetcar. Hence the name, "streetcar college." Some of us, including me, simply walked across the street to the campus, while others moved readily in and out on mass transit. Then, as now, there is a difference between walking onto the campus at the University of Cincinnati, and walking into the heart of a smaller school campus such as Princeton University, where I teach. UC's campus edge is ragged, not well defined except on the main street, McMicken Street.

However, what happened to UC happened to many campuses throughout the country in the 1960s and 1970s. The student body expanded exponentially. The University of Cincinnati became a state university in 1977, and by this time the student population had grown from approximately 7,000 when I attended, to some 40,000 persons. As was occurring everywhere, there was little time to plan the new "mega" buildings that seemed to be needed, and limited funds meant that the quality of construction suffered enormously. During this same time, UC the streetcar college became a commuter college with the majority of students driving cars to campus and needing to park. Multi-level parking garages went up. Imagine Oxford or Cambridge trying to absorb a number of those. Well, that is in fact what did happen to UC: the campus of rather gentle Georgian beginnings fastforwarded into giant parking structures.

Another challenge was topographical. The UC campus stands on a series of small hills, which has made identifying *the place*—a unity—difficult.

My thought has always been rather than attempting to make a unified campus, one should instead play to the idea of little villages-different colleges loosely connected within separate precincts. They could be linked by the landscape, or by communal activities. These goals are what the university has been recently looking to achieve in implementing ambitious, parallel projects: the 1991 Hargreaves master plan, and the selection of "signature architects" to design individual buildings.

Now, with some hindsight, one is anxious to put Humpty Dumpty back together again. There is an attempt to reduce the effect of existing buildings that are out of scale by clever planning and intelligent landscape design. Not much can be done at this point about such regrettable physical changes as the severing of the campus from Burnet Woods by the widening of Martin Luther King, perhaps, but much thoughtful work is being done to create urban spaces that link buildings already on the campus, such as the Library Plaza or the Campus Green. Overlaid with the creation of a continuous, landscaped route through the campus has been the building of signature architectural designs; you will judge for yourself their success as "infill" or "background" buildings. What matters is that my alma mater, whose School of Medicine housed virologist Albert Sabin and which has one of the best archaeology departments I know, has arisen like a phoenix from the ashes, to deserve this Campus Guide and your visit.

Michael Graves, FAIA
University of Cincinnati, BS in Architecture, 1958
February 2001

Engineering Research Center and Crosley Tower

Introduction to the University of Cincinnati

The University of Cincinnati presents the lover of architecture with two extremes: examples of some of the best architecture in the world, coupled with even more examples of really bad architecture. It is, of course, the great architecture that has prompted this book and that will be continuously emphasized throughout (if not trumpeted). But in order to fully understand the importance of these select works, and how the university has become in a very short time one of the more important destinations for world class architecture, one must really spend some time looking at the bad architecture first.

When Alexis de Tocqueville arrived in Cincinnati by steamer in 1832 he noted in his journal how the frenzied pace, driven by commerce on the Ohio River, made life here seem haphazard and disordered. "[It] presents an odd spectacle," the philosopher noted. "A town which seems to want to get built too quickly to have things done in order." One hundred and fifty years later he might have said the same thing for the city's academic institution. By the 1980s the University of Cincinnati had become a disordered place. Buildings had been erected at a quickened pace with no great plan, practically since the institution was founded back in 1870. With some exceptions, the architecture was poor, at times inhospitable, and generally uninspiring. Worst of all was the burden of cars, which somehow had found their way into the center of campus. Instead of a large campus green, the symbol of American education, UC's heart was paved for parking. It was demoralizing.

In 1984, the tide began to change with the entry on the scene of a new president, Joseph Steger. Steger understood that the poorly planned campus held several consequences for the university, not the least of which was financial. If the place looked bad, how could he ever attract new donors, or important faculty and researchers, or even more importantly students? In sum, with a parking lot in the middle of the campus and old, ugly buildings, why would anyone ever love the University of Cincinnati? And without love and alumni devotion where was UC? Not that all the buildings on campus were ugly. In fact, despite the fact that the current planners of the university universally despise anything built before 1990, there are several "bad" buildings that are really quite wonderful. Part of the purpose of this guide is to help you decide which is which, and why.

A Bit of History

The University of Cincinnati traces its history to the ambitious dreams of an ambitious nineteenth-century Cincinnatian, who, in the pages of history, seems to have walked right out of Tocqueville's own description of the city. Daniel Drake was a child of the frontier, born to two New Jersey travelers on their way west for a better life. As a young man he apprenticed with the only doctor in the fledgling settlement of Cincinnati, a New Yorker appropriately named William Goforth, who sent his young charge back east to acquire a formal education from the University of Pennsylvania. Upon Drake's return to Cincinnati in 1807 he took over Goforth's practice and settled into life as a doctor in the growing town.

But there was little settled about Drake. He is described as a kind of "frontier Leonardo" in the history books, and by the time he was thirty had published books on the culture of the west, completed statistical studies of the new city, and been bit by a bug to establish a medical college in Cincinnati. With some political bargaining he obtained a charter from the state of Ohio to develop the Medical College of Ohio, which opened for business in 1819. Three days earlier, coincidentally, the legislature had also issued a charter for a general academic institution called the Cincinnati College and charged the Reverend Elijah Slack, a Pennsylvanian come west, with its management. In short time Drake ran afoul of the faculty of his new school and jumped ship to Cincinnati College to found another medical college there. His efforts came to naught, but he did persuade the legislature to fund what he called an "academic department" in the school, which we now call a liberal arts school. Drake then disappeared and the Medical College and Cincinnati College (which soon boasted a law school) went on happily in their respective trajectories for the next fifty years. During that time numerous other small colleges with greater and lesser success were founded in the rapidly growing city, including the Ohio Mechanics Institute (an engineering school) and the Conservatory of Music.

The lake in Burnet Woods

In 1858 Charles McMicken, a business and real estate magnate who owned a lot of land in the city, died. In his will, after providing for his heirs, he bequeathed almost all of his property to Cincinnati for the purpose of establishing what he called "Cincinnati University." Where this quiet, taciturn man ever dreamed up such a scheme is lost to history; but after several years of legal wrangling, the university was opened for business. Housed in a small building downtown, the university at first boasted little more than a night school and a drawing college. But in 1885, a business-minded fellow by the name of Jacob Cox was selected president of the school and set about trying to incorporate a number of small colleges in the city into it. Over the next eighty years one by one the Medical College of Ohio, the Ohio Mechanics Institute, the Conservatory, and many other specialized colleges were absorbed into what indeed became a real university. Today those early schools form the colleges of medicine, engineering, and music—the cornerstone academic programs at UC.

In 1875 the first building of the university was constructed, next door to McMicken's estate, on Vine Street between Clifton Avenue and what today is called McMicken Avenue. The site chosen was on a slope and thus earned the school the appellation "the hilltop university." This building was a tall, broad-shouldered Victorian manor house, with a dramatic sloping roof punctuated by dormers and distinguished chimneys. It was also a dirty, soot-filled place that by the 1880s had been enveloped by industrial neighborhoods. Cox petitioned to move the school farther up the hill, to a place still called Burnet Woods. He succeeded, and in 1895 a new home for the

Power building and smokestack

THE UNIVERSITY OF CINCINNATI IN THE TWENTIETH CENTURY

A SUGGESTION
OCTOBER, 1898

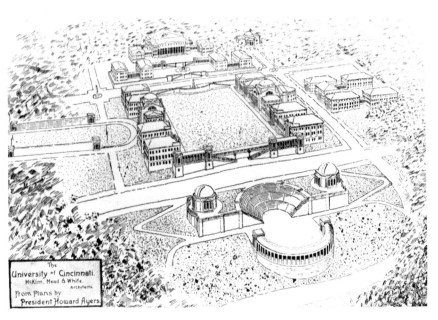

TOP: *Proposed campus plan, 1898*
BOTTOM: *Proposed campus plan, 1904*

university was constructed on a ridge along Clifton Avenue and named for
the original benefactor of the University. This first McMicken Hall was
designed by Samuel Hannaford, at the time the leading architect in
Cincinnati and firmly in the pocket of the local political bosses. Hannaford's
was a graceful neo-Georgian structure with two flanking wings that, along
with Hannaford's two downtown masterpieces, City Hall and Music Hall,
formed part of his enormous legacy in Cincinnati.

During the first thirty years of its life, the campus was both haphazard and regular in its growth. The regularity concerned style. Following
Hannaford's lead, most of the buildings designed on campus adhered

Memorial Dormitory, now part of the CCM Village

roughly to the neo-Georgian style. UC's use of the Georgian style—as opposed to the Collegiate Gothic style then in vogue at many schools and universities around the country (notably Yale and its knockoffs)—referenced Thomas Jefferson and the early days of the republic. The term Georgian, of course, refers to King George whom the colonialists refuted and revolted against, so it is a little misleading as a term applied to American architecture. But, generally speaking, the American interpretation of this English style had a calm, less decorative aspect, with a few solid references to classical architecture (namely, Roman) in the form of pediments, cornices, and use of inscriptions. Probably the most famously Georgian campus (he would have hated the term—he called it an "academical village") is Jefferson's University of Virginia. UC's appropriation of the style, and "neo" updating of it in the early decades of the century, was an overt sign that the university wanted to position itself not only as an important municipal or even regional institution, but as an inherently American and national academy. It was an Americanism of the most respected sort: handsome, not flashy.

Despite this regularity in style, the planning of the campus occurred haphazardly. At first, new buildings were laid out along the ridge in a line with McMicken Hall. This so-called "academic ridge" was fairly unusual for the time, as most campuses around the country were being built in the Beaux-Arts style, as balanced quadrangles centered on tree-studded greens. In some ways

TOP: *Detail from Blegen Library*
BOTTOM: *Reading room, Blegen Library, circa 1940*

Dyer Hall

UC's linear plan was a functional response to the existence of a streetcar line that once ran up Clifton Avenue and which brought, even at this early time, many of the young commuting students up to the school from downtown. Concurrently with the build-out on the ridge, however, the university also embarked on the construction of a Beaux Arts quad—called Baldwin Quad and anchored by Baldwin Hall (1911), which housed the engineering college. Although formally quite traditional, with buildings balancing one another in a perfect rectangle and an open green in the middle, the orientation of this quad was, quite bizarrely, canted off axis from the original ridge, introducing not only a new planning form to the campus but an entirely new orientation for the future construction of buildings. To complicate matters further, the lowland area behind the ridge had been used for recreation for years, and in 1912 was formally so dedicated by the construction of a stadium. This structure was placed to conform to the natural topography and thus laid out at yet another angle to the ridge. In quick succession two new halls—Schmidlapp (now Dieterle) and Memorial Hall—were built in the same manner, all of which established a whole new pattern of building. So it remained up to World War II, as new buildings were erected at a steady pace and the university increasingly looked like three different campuses conjoined in a haphazard way.

In 1911 the College of Medicine built a new home for itself a short distance to the northeast of the academic ridge. This new teaching hospital would form the backbone for the East Campus. A slight hill and the inter-section of what would turn out to be two very busy roads gradually served to create a barrier between this new or East Campus and the original or West Campus. In many ways (culturally, architecturally) the two campuses would evolve differently.

Postwar Blues

Like most other schools in the country, building pretty much ceased at UC during World War II. Afterwards, flush with G.I. Bill students, the university scrambled to grow. New buildings were constructed at a breakneck pace, and as a result little thought was given to their placement. At the same time, the old neo-Georgian standard was abandoned in favor of a kind of debased modernism that, with some exceptions, confused the aesthetic presentation of campus. In some instances, new buildings showcased bizarre and unusual decorative motifs. And by the 1960s there was a movement toward construct-ing very large towers with little or no connection to the local context. But as despised as many of these buildings are today, such value judgments are noto-riously fickle; and in some instances there are some wonderful gems amidst these hulking beasts that, one hopes, will be discovered and preserved.

After World War II, the modern university was born. Several of the early colleges began to grow and develop into nationally recognized

Aerial view of West Campus, circa 1940

programs. These included the engineering school, the music school, and
several medical research programs. The sports programs also gained force,
and fieldhouse and field facilities were expanded in the center of campus to
nurture future stars. As the university grew, however, it remained very much
a commuter school, with the vast majority of the students arriving every day
by car. This forced the campus to develop extensive parking facilities.
Almost without exception these were designed and built without sensitivity.
Large garages erected by engineering firms hulked around the perimeter
and in some cases became visual eyesores. But the biggest problem lay in the
surface lots that filled the inner core of the campus. In the middle of West
Campus, instead of a bucolic village green students looked upon a sea of
cars; while opposite, at the entrance to East Campus, was a dusty dirt lot.
Things were pretty grim.

      Although we tend to look at the mundane architectural styles as the
most visible legacy of this postwar boom, it was the lack of planning and
placement of buildings without forethought that created the most havoc at
UC. Without a plan in mind, the university simply plopped buildings down
willy nilly, sometimes emphasizing one orientation line or another, or more
often simply ignoring any of the three oddly related existing building patterns
and introducing new ones. The worst cases were the skyscraper towers that
were placed in the middle of a site and then ringed by parking lots, of which
the university built several in conspicuous places. The construction of Sander
Hall, a twenty-seven-story monolith that dominated campus visually and
spiritually for twenty years, represents pinnacle of this folly. It was constructed in 1970 and fairly well despised from the beginning. The elevators
couldn't handle the capacity; the local neighborhood thought it an affront to
their quaint house-lined streets; and when several students attempted suicide

Implosion of Sander Hall, 1991

by jumping from the top, a dark shadow was cast over Sander. In 1991, in front of more than twenty thousand onlookers, the hall was imploded and reduced to dust. It was an act of violence that presaged a sea change at UC.

The change had begun in 1984, when Joseph Steger became president of the university. Steger, a pragmatic but visionary man, immediately understood that for all the positive attributes of the university—its status as a leading research institution, its successful athletics program, and its position as the leading academic institution in the region—the physical campus was in shambles and communicated a poor message to outsiders. The word he used was "polyglot," which implied a centerless, soulless place; the campus was too much of everything and nothing at the same time. What it desperately needed was an identifiable image. One of the first things Steger did was organize a planning committee, headed by himself.

Dale McGirr, vice president of finance, immediately put all building plans on hold until a vision for the campus could be articulated. Steger agreed. For this they decided to hire a master planner. They hoped to find someone versed in college planning, who could understand the predicament the university had gotten itself into, and who could offer unique, potentially transformative solutions. It was this last bit that became the stickler as the committee began interviewing planners. While there certainly was no shortage of good campus planners out there, few had any really dramatic prescriptives for how the campus might change. Except one. On a lark, Steger had inserted the name of landscape architect George Hargreaves into the list of planners to interview. Hargreaves, although respected as a designer, had little experience as a planner, and certainly had never worked on a project of this scale before. He'd prepared some sketches of ideas for how to convert the large parking lot in the middle of the West Campus into a landscaped green. And Steger thought he might be able to offer an entirely different perspective.

Hargreaves and his partner, landscape architect Mary Margaret Jones, presented a very different vision than the competition. While the architects and master planners were offering individual remedies—moving this road here, that parking lot there—Hargreaves proposed radically re-envisioning the entire campus. What really made the campus, they argued, was the feeling of having a single experience. That you could walk through and everywhere feel like you were somewhere. And in order to do this UC needed to look beyond just architecture. It needed to see the total environment—the landscape, the architecture, and how these two interacted to create, in Gestalt fashion, something greater.

The Hargreaves master plan, which was accepted in 1991, basically proposed three things. The first was that all new building needed to be thought of in terms of infill. Instead of colonizing some new space and placing a building in the middle of it, the new architecture of the school needed to be fitted into the existing fabric of the campus, no matter how "polyglot" that fabric might be. The core of this idea rested on an analysis of how the university had developed along conflicting lines of orientation, which Jones and Hargreaves termed "force fields." They wanted to emphasize these force fields and use them as architectural inspiration. In some ways, Hargreaves was telling the university that its odd architectural history might actually be an asset. In an architectural sense, "infill" buildings are very different than traditional buildings. Instead of existing as objects in space that can be viewed from all sides like a monument or sculpture, infill architecture is generally three sided or two sided, with the other sides acting less as parts of an object and more as boundaries or walls that shape and carve space. Not surprisingly, this is an idea that comes from landscape architecture and not from the traditional fields of architecture and planning.

The second major proposal of Hargreaves' plan was to use architecture primarily as way to create open space. UC is not a land-rich place, and the practice of placing buildings in the middle of open spaces had resulted in the reduction of open space available for students to hang out, play Frisbee, or do any of the other things that are critical to creating a culture on campus. New buildings needed to be pressed into tighter, denser, configurations to open large swaths of land and also to create urban-scaled courtyards and plazas of a different sort. The idea was to think of the university as a variety of interior and exterior spaces that feed into one another and are intensely habitable while not being mundane. Another of the ills of the commuter campus was that, after five, the campus became a ghost town. The campus needed spaces that could be programmed with activity: restaurants, cafes, theaters, and other amenities, enveloped by an architecture that was functional and beautiful.

The last idea proposed by the Hargreaves plan was to develop a network of landscape spaces that wound through the campus like a green spine and promoted the idea of walking between the East and West Campuses. The idea, derived from Frederick Law Olmsted's nineteenth-century plan for Boston Parks ("the Emerald Necklace"), was dubbed "a string of pearls," and when completed would connect McMicken Hall to the College of Medicine. The goal was to increase the amount of inhabitable landscape on campus by twenty-five percent when done.

At the same time that Hargreaves was working on the master plan, Jayanta ("Jay") Chatterjee, Dean of the College of Design, Architecture, Art, and Planning, was working on his own parallel initiative. The College of Design, Art, Architecture, and Planning, known as the DAAP, needed a new home. While all building plans were on hold, he proposed a new direction for the design and construction of new architecture. Instead of hiring a local architect to erect yet another building on campus, why not look for a big-name, internationally-recognized "signature" architect to come to UC and design a building that would turn heads? The way he saw it, such a move would both create a stir and draw attention to the university (something very much desired by the administrators trying to market the school), and it would also represent a real attempt to solve some of the architectural problems on campus. Chatterjee describes this time in the mid-1980s as a moment of intense demoralization within the DAAP. "Instead of developing plans for how the campus might look with new buildings, we were working renderings that purposely excluded certain buildings, in essence arguing that the campus would look better in many cases without existing architecture."

After clearing several bureaucratic hurdles, most notably the mandate of using Ohio architects on a state-funded institution (which he surmounted by agreeing to use a local architect as a "architect of record" who would implement the design), Chatterjee invited ten leading architects to visit the school and make presentations: Frank Gehry, Michael Graves, Charles Gwathmey, Peter Eisenman, Cesar Pelli, and half a dozen other notable architects—the likes of which hadn't been seen on campus before. It was a watershed event. As Sander Hall crumbled on one part of campus, this group huddled in a poorly lit lecture hall concocting schemes for a new vision.

Signature Architecture
The selection of Peter Eisenman for the DAAP building heralded a new era for UC. It was followed by that of Michael Graves, David Childs, Henry Cobb, Frank Gehry, Machado and Silvetti, and Cambridge Seven for a sequence of other important commissions, all of which by 2000 had been built. Other important buildings are under construction or in the works by Leers Weinzapfel, Gwathmey Siegel, Moore Rubbel Yudel, and Morphosis—all forward-looking, internationally recognized firms. The effect has been transformative. Ten years ago, the campus was a motley assortment of banal buildings. Today is a veritable museum of architecture. Where else can you see a major work by Frank Gehry in proximity to piece by Peter Eisenman? Or a Henry Cobb building within a stone's throw of a Gwathmey Siegel and Leers Weinzapfel? The short answer is nowhere.

For the architects themselves UC has become a playground of innovation. Greg Karn, the project manager at Gwathmey Siegel—the firm

The Main Street proposal

designing the new student union on campus—says that because the university is so enthusiastic about good architecture and because he finds himself working alongside other important architects with good ideas, it's "almost like being on sabbatical." Essentially what UC is creating is a forum for architectural dialogue. In most cases this is a long-term conversation, occurring over a space of time when a new structure is built in the vicinity of others and comparisons can be made. But in the case of the new Main Street, where you have four prominent firms working on buildings adjacent to one another at the same time, with the landscape architects Mary Margaret Jones and George Hargreaves sitting in the middle acting as a kind of go-between and moderator—but also executing their own original design for the unifying sequence of open spaces between them, the dialogue becomes real-time. In fact, while the university pursues yet more polyglot architecture (this of an artistic nature), the landscape architect George Hargreaves' work has established a kind of visual linkage through the campus; he has designed all of the string of pearls thus far completed. These landscape spaces, which with the completion of Main Street will extend from McMicken Commons to the intersection between the campus halves, are all of a piece and form a skein of continuity through the increasingly complex, if clarified, campus. While the look and feel of the campus is new, provocative, and exciting, in many ways the approach is quite traditional. Like the great campuses of the past, UC is relying on the subtle power of landscape design to create a sense of place and unity, what is being touted as "an identifiable image" for the campus. As a result, while we are wowed by the excellent buildings, it is the landscape—a pastiche of molded landforms, non-Euclidean walkways, and sparse plantings—that is making the university a cohesive place.

The great hope of architecture since the Enlightenment is that the environment, in this case the spaces we inhabit, can be manipulated to make us better. In this view architecture is seen as the great nurturer, a surrogate parent of sorts or a teacher, which influences our mind and spirit as much as it houses our body. Somewhere in the kernel of all built spaces, even the most cynical ones, lies this idea. But in the contemporary world nowhere is it expressed more fully than in the educational setting of the American campus.

The University of Cincinnati campus, while wildly on the cutting edge in terms of planning, landscape, and architectural design, fits neatly within this paradigm. Like all great campuses, there is a latent faith in its new direction that architecture can actually mold better people. This isn't to say, exactly, that Michael Graves' Engineering Research Building will actually turn out better engineering students, or that Peter Eisenman's DAAP building will make for better architects. It's broader than that. The question is, as Rousseau may have put it, will these architectural monuments make better citizens? One key figure in the planning effort, Dale McGirr, the vice-president of finance at UC, described it this way. He said that the new architecture of UC was intended to create a *forum* and *language* for living—two parallel notions: one Socratic in spirit, the other Wittgensteinian. He hopes, as does the university as a whole, that good design can actually transform life, and that this investment in remaking the university in an inventive way will pay intellectual dividends in the students that it produces.

If the philosophy stems from the Enlightenment, the process is pure Italian Renaissance. People like Chatterjee, McGirr, and Steger are the consummate patrons.

Original Campus and College of Design, Architecture, Art, and Planning (DAAP)

1 | McMicken Hall
2 | Administration Building
3 | a) Teachers College
  | b) Dyer Hall
4 | Carl Blegen Library
5 | College of Law
6 | Across Clifton:
  | a) Hughes High School
  | b) Hillel
7 | Wilson Auditorium
8 | a) Alms Building
  | b) Wolfson Hall
  | c) Design, Architecture, Art, and Planning (DAAP)
  | d) Aronoff Center for Design and Art

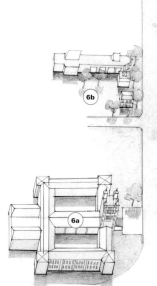

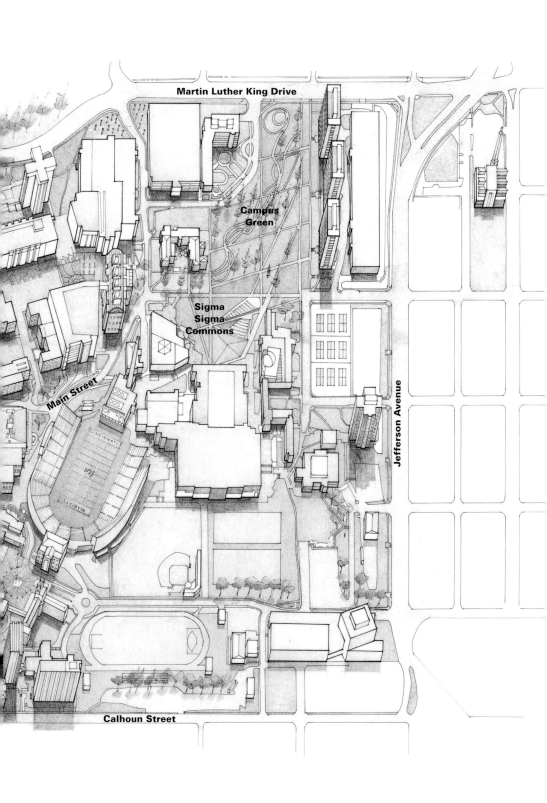

Martin Luther King Drive

Campus
Green

Sigma
Sigma
Commons

Main Street

Jefferson Avenue

CINCINNATI

Calhoun Street

From the Academic Ridge to DAAP

The oldest buildings on campus are situated along a ridge that runs parallel to Clifton Avenue, the so-called academical ridge in knowing reference to Jefferson's "academical village" at the University of Virginia. The connections go beyond the euphemism. The older buildings, which were designed and built between 1895 and 1940, all conform to the Georgian style dominant at UVA. The idea was to connect the University of Cincinnati, then a fledgling regional institution, to the larger context of American universities by choosing an architectural style that was both patriotic and identifiably "academic" to the outsider. McMicken Hall, which is actually the last in a series of three McMicken Halls, forms the cornerstone of this philosophy. The one we see today was designed by Harry Hake, the most prolific Cincinnati architect on campus, and strikes a modest chord. Farther along the ridge, forming a line, we find Teacher's College and Dyer Hall, as well Taft Hall (now ensconced within the larger College of Law building), all uniformly designed with similar red brick facing, limestone trim, and neoclassical detailing—although the elaborateness of this detailing varies from building to building as we progress through history. Beyond the ridge, the Georgian ideal was extended outward as the university grew—most specifically to the Baldwin Quad (see Walk Three); however after World War II, when the campus grew at a rapid pace, the traditional approach lost favor to more modernist styles.

Between the brick Georgian buildings are several stone-faced neoclassical structures—the two libraries (Van Wormer and Blegen) and Wilson Auditorium. These structures provide a neat counterpoint to McMicken Hall and the others, creating a kind of relief in the homogeneity of brick. But they are not anomalies. Each of these structures (designed between 1899 and 1931) were suited to specific purposes within the university and thus were intended to have architectures that contrasted—albeit within the same classical theme.

The abandonment of neo-Georgian brick took place around 1950, as the university sought to create a more functional, contemporary, and seemingly urban setting. At the end of this first Walk, as Clifton Avenue slopes down to Martin Luther King Drive, we come across two of the finer modernist buildings at DAAP, as well as the first in a series of "signature buildings" that are rapidly defining the university. The new Aronoff Center for Design and Architecture, designed by Peter Eisenman and completed in 1996, made a major impact on the architectural scene worldwide and is one of that architect's most admired works. It sits at the edge of the campus, before the land slopes off into the unkempt bramble of Burnet Woods, like a harbinger of the new life that Jay Chatterjee, president Joseph Steger, and master planner George Hargreaves are breathing into the campus. Although designed prior to the articulation of the master plan, the building addresses the mandate that architecture on the campus should be seen as infill—forming space rather than consuming it. Eisenman's entire scheme was predicated on the existing malformation of three disparate buildings, something that most architects would view as a mistake of history, but which he saw as inspiration. This irregular geometry—the chevron—was abstracted into a complex of many different irregular geometries, churned through the computer to create a building where no two angles are the same.

One wants to describe this first Walk as the most cohesive of the seven Walks in this guide, in that the majority of the buildings all hark from the pre-war period when the driving force in campus development was toward a consistent neo-Georgian style. While this is true to some extent, the center does not hold, so to speak. Even with McMicken Hall, the most forceful expression of the neo-Georgian aesthetic, we find a palimpsest—a building that has been written over a previous building. There is no pure architectural space on the campus of the University of Cincinnati. There is no one building that remains unchanged. And instead, all have at one time or another been in flux. If change, then, is the constant in this rapidly reinventing place, then it seems that Walk One, which traverses more than a century of architecture, should provide the right kind of start.

1. McMicken Hall *Hake & Hake, 1948*

McMicken Hall is the spiritual epicenter of campus. Named after Charles McMicken, the Cincinnati businessman who donated the land for the university in 1858, the hall that stands today replaced an earlier structure designed by Samuel Hannaford, who had studied classical architecture under John R. Hamilton and was, by the late nineteenth century, the most prominent architect in Cincinnati. Today, he is remembered as the designer of Music Hall, City Hall, and Memorial Hall, all of which are located downtown and attest to Hannaford's absolute versatility and eclectic style. He could, it was said, design almost anything in almost any style. Hannaford's McMicken Hall, which was erected in 1894 and dismantled in 1948, was a decorative neoclassical structure with a thin, undersized tower, festooned with carved Greek sculptures and flanked by magnificent marble stairs. Essentially, the floor plan and siting of the building Hannaford established are the same today, replicated in the modern building. There was a central hall flanked by two wings, each named after early benefactors of the school—philanthropist Henry Hanna and Briggs Cunningham, a member of the university's board of directors. At the time of its construction in 1894 the Academic Department, a euphemism for the College of Arts and Sciences,

was housed here. Seminar rooms were on the top floor, with a gymnasium in the basement and library on the ground floor.

In 1948, Hannaford's outdated structure was torn down, and local architect Harry Hake was charged with designing a replacement. Like Hannaford fifty years earlier, Hake was at this time one of the most prominent architects in Cincinnati. He too had been classically trained and was known for his ability to work in a variety of styles, depending on the tastes of his clients and the signs of the times. For McMicken Hall he took a much simpler approach than Hannaford. The basic structure, lying as it does on the footprint of the earlier building, is the same, with a central hall flanked by two wings, again dedicated to Hanna and Cunningham. But gone are the excessive decorations. The trim, executed in bright white Indiana limestone, lacks detail and instead provides contrast for the light brick facing. The style is colonial or Georgian, which Hake obviously understood as conforming to a specific tradition of American campus architecture—most notably the Jeffersonian (he would have rejected the term "Georgian") architecture of the University of Virginia. Unlike Yale or Princeton, with their Collegiate Gothic, and hence very European, architectures, the University of Virginia was a quintessentially American place—refined, somewhat humble, but quite beautiful. It is fair to assume that Hake and his patron, then-president Dr. Raymond Walters, with the war in Europe just ended and the University of Cincinnati growing by leaps, wanted to make a patriotic statement that wasn't too regionally specific. Their McMicken Hall would be a part of a larger, homespun tradition—the University of Cincinnati would be a national university.

Hake's tower, symbolically rising above the rest of campus, was inspired by Christopher Wren's tower at the College of William and Mary, which in turn was derived from St. Paul's Cathedral in London. It is well proportioned against the facade. 650,000 bricks from the old Hall were reused in the construction. Flanking the arched entryway that bisects the surprisingly narrow central hall are two stone lions, donated by Jacob Hoffner and affectionately nicknamed Mick and Mack. They were placed in front of the original hall in 1904. In 1971 vandals hacked them apart, and when they were reassembled no one could remember which was Mack and vice versa. Above the lions, etched into the facade, is the anonymous quotation of nonsense pragmatism that one feels throughout the campus and culture of the university: "Wisdom is the principal thing. Therefore get wisdom."

OPPOSITE: *McMicken Hall*

Administration Building

2. Administration Building *Samuel Hannaford & Sons, 1899*

The Administration Building, originally called the Van Wormer Library, is the oldest building on campus. It was designed by Samuel Hannaford & Sons in 1899 at time when the elder Hannaford was preparing to retire from the firm, and his sons, Charles and Harvey, were taking over. The style, making reference to the municipal libraries funded by Andrew Carnegie all across America as well as to Columbia's Low library, is Greek classical—or, to be more precise, a Roman interpretation of the classical Greek form, which generally speaking is a more rigid, formal, and secular vision of Greek architecture. The building sits on the academical ridge of the original campus as a square mass of stone, which in design and original construction sported a small, inspired dome, humble in its proportions. Today, the dome-less roofline looks strangely flat, as if aching for complement. Two large Ionic columns, which flank the entrance, alleviate the square proportions of the building. Inside, the structure was laid out as a large open rotunda with stacks revolving around the central airy vortex. In 1930, when a new library was built a few doors down (now the Blegen Library), the Van Wormer was converted into offices for the school administration. The open space was filled in with floors, although you can still sense the general feel of the building on the ground floor where office spaces are arranged around a large central space. The detailing from the original building still exists in some parts, including the marble entry and attractive iron lamps and iron grillwork in the lobby. The Van Wormer may seem out of place on the academic ridge

Teachers College

and the university in general; its cold stone facade and classical decorations don't jibe with the softer brick tones and understated Georgian details of the various academic buildings. In the history of campus architecture, however, this contrast is perfectly in step. The library, especially this early one, was seen as a kind of fortress for books, to protect them not only from fire and other natural threats, but also to entomb them in a way. The idea was to create a holy place for books where a kind of priestly class of knowledge seekers might study sheltered from the outside world.

3. Teachers College and Dyer Hall

Teachers College *Garber & Woodward, 1930*
Dyer Hall *Garber & Woodward, 1931*
Connector *Cyrus Baxter, 1958*

Teachers College and Dyer Hall were originally designed in 1930 by Frederick Garber and Clifford Woodward as sister structures. They were joined in 1958 by a connector wing designed by local architect Cyrus Baxter to create a kind of half-quad, open on the northern end. Besides being partners, Garber and Woodward were brothers-in-law and shared a common sensibility about Georgian architectural styles. Both of their buildings here are characterized by scaled-down neoclassical features such as pilaster columns and relief sculpture. Architectural historian Walter E.

Langsam notes that Garber and Woodward were well versed in the under-pinnings of American colonial architecture; in particular they had studied the work of English neoclassical architect Robert Adam. The thin, flat pilasters and split arches, remarks Langsam, are almost "Adamesque." The enormous sandstone eagles and owls were carved by Lee Lawrie, a notable Cincinnati sculptor who worked with John Russell Pope and Cass Gilbert on buildings downtown. In contrast with these Roman motifs Garber and Woodward gave the buildings simple, modern detailing in terms of the trim lines that run the length of the building uninterrupted and the lack of sculptural adornment near to the roofline. Above the southern entrance to Teachers College are several wonderfully Art Deco windows with intriguing abstract designs. The buildings were originally used to house the natural sciences, evidenced by the inscriptions "Zoology," "Pharmacy," and "Botany" above the doors. The interior of the two halls and their connector are rather run of the mill, especially in the connector, which (intentionally it seems) looks straight out of most suburban high schools, right down to the lockers, intended to create the atmosphere of a real school for education students.

4. Carl Blegen Library

Hake & Kuck, 1930; Burgess & Niple Limited, Architects, interior redesign, 1980

In 1927 the university commissioned Harry Hake, a rising star in Cincinnati architecture, to design a new library almost next door to the existing Van Wormer Library (see Administration Building above) along the academic ridge of the campus. The new building was also designed in the Greek Revival style, with a series of inscriptions and bas-reliefs carved into its facade that represent the pursuit of knowledge. Within the parapet above the door, the scene represents modern civilization (the female figure) as the product of Eastern and Western intellectual history, represented by the Hebrew and Latin words for light and various symbols of knowledge, such as an Assyrian winged lion, a medieval castle, and so on. Below the fifth floor windows (the second floor when viewed from here on the western side of the building) are two panels representing great thinkers and scholars from the two traditions. To the right, the southern side of the doorway, we see (from right to left) Sargon the Great, Cheops (seated with a model of his pyramid in his lap), Hammurabi, Moses (with tablets), Darius the Great, Confucius, Buddha, Jesus, and Justinian. The Latin inscription below trans-lates as "Light from the East." To the left, north, of the doorway we see great thinkers from the western tradition represented—with the parallel inscription, "Light from the West." They are, from left to right, Euclid, Homer (with a lyre), Phidias, Plato, Herodotus, Shakespeare, Goethe,

Blegen Library

Blegen Library

Galileo, and Dante. In the doorway of the library are two groups of bronzes, sculpted by George Marshall Martin, employed by the Hake architectural firm, depicting Minerva (above the door) and a series of bas-reliefs that tell the story of bookmaking. The theme of bookmaking can be found throughout the library. On the window grills along ground level are various printers marks from important book-makers. The building itself is set into the side of the ridge, and the main entrance on the western side opens into the fourth-floor level. Originally the interior was marked by a large open rotunda, surrounded by rooms. The stacks were constructed out of cast iron, an innovation in library design at the time as it allowed for greater air circulation around the books and reduced mold. In 1978 the general collection was removed to the new library across campus and the interior of the structure was redesigned to accommodate a variety of offices, including the Archives & Rare Books division. The voluminous entrance hall was divided up into floors to make it more useful, and with the exception of the moldings, chandeliers, and general sense of how the space was once divided, the former majesty of the building's interior is gone. At the time of its remodeling the library was renamed after archeology professor Carl Blegen, whose work on the ancient sites of Troy and Pylos was seminal.

5. College of Law

Taft Hall *Harry Hake, 1925*
Marx Library *Herbert Hilmer, 1965*

The original college of law was designed by the ubiquitous Harry Hake, who also designed Tangeman Center, McMicken Hall, and a host of other buildings on campus in the interwar period. This college building, like those others, was crafted in a neo-Georgian style. It was dedicated to Alphonso Taft, an alumnus of the college and later its dean. In the late 1970s the American Bar Association threatened to revoke the college's accreditation if it did not substantially expand the building. The college hired Cincinnati architect Herbert Hilmer to complete the addition. Instead of adding a wing or in

College of Law

some way appending a new building to the old, Hilmer decided to strip the facade of the old building, including the massive hollow columns, and wrap a new structure around it. The result is an airy, sky-lit walkway that winds around the old structure, serving to highlight the rich, soft-colored brick exterior. On the outside of this are a series of offices and classrooms. The old Taft Hall was converted into lecture halls and mock courtrooms. The most notable change is the addition of a multilevel law library, dedicated to Robert S. Marx, also an alumnus of the college and a judge in Cincinnati. From the exterior, Hilmer's "wrap" presents itself as a series of rectangular boxes, set one upon another in the modernist idiom, and punctuated along their length by recesses and windows that alleviate the apparent weight of the mass. A sensitivity to scale and to the integration of landscape is shown in the way the building sinks into the berm on its west (Clifton Avenue) face. After twenty years the shade trees, grown into maturity, create the interplay between the organic forms of nature and the austere manmade forms that were the ideal of such modernists as Mies van der Rohe and Frank Lloyd Wright. Behind the College of Law lies a small courtyard with a statue of the wonderfully mustachioed Taft, regal and imposing and eight feet tall. It was sculpted by Michael D. Bigger and put here in 1991.

Hughes High School

Hillel: The Rose Warner House

6. Across Clifton

Hughes High School *J. Walter Stevens, 1908*
Hillel: The Rose Warner House *Architekton, 1982*

On your way down Clifton Avenue to visit the next building on campus in
this Walk, cross to the western side of the street and visit two notable
buildings that, while not strictly a part of campus, do contribute to its architectural context. The first is the massive Hughes High School, located on
the corner of Calhoun Street and Clifton Avenue, across from the College
of Law. The story goes that the local architecture association became frus-
trated with how design commissions were being doled out by corrupt
politicians (mostly to the firm of Samuel Hannaford) and petitioned to hold
a real design competition for this structure shortly after the turn of the century. To their dismay J. Walter Stevens from St. Paul, Minnesota—not a
local architect—won the competition, effectively ending the drive to liberal-
ize the architectural commissioning process for some time. Stevens' design
falls neatly into the Collegiate Gothic style, with pretty faithful stylizations
in the frightening gargoyles. The massive scale of the site surely must have
terrified young students. Farther down Clifton Avenue is the Jewish student center Hillel, also known as the Rose Warner House. It was designed
in 1982 by local firm Architekton. The facade of the one-story structure
walks back from the street in a jagged line allowing for a massive linear
grove of thin-leafed honey locusts. The multi-pyramidal roofline looks like
two saltbox houses meeting in space. The building houses the Jewish

student organization Hillel. The tapestries in the temple are Hungarian and were confiscated by the Nazis during World War II, while the rest of the artifacts are all from old synagogues in the city that have since closed as the Jewish population has declined, despite the fact that this is the home of reform Judaism. Architecturally, the dual kitchens for the kosher separation of meat and dairy represent the most intriguing feature; they share a wall and form a divided square between them: a wonderfully articulated example of this spiritual precept.

7. Wilson Auditorium *Fechheimer & Ihorst, 1931*

Wilson Auditorium

Wilson Auditorium was designed by A. Lincoln Fechheimer, one of the first Jewish architects in the city, and his partner Benjamin Ihorst. Fechheimer was only the second Cincinnatian to attend the formidable École de Beaux Arts in Paris, the leading architecture school of the day, and his intense study of classical forms is apparent in the Roman Imperial stylizing of this exterior. But strictness to the Roman (and their adherence to Greek) forms is forfeited in certain places in favor of simpler, more *moderne* touches. The brick pattern of alternating large and small bricks, for instance, has an almost Art Deco sensibility. As do the bas-relief sculptures that depict figures from the Enlightenment such as Molière, Webster, and Burke. The four muses of the arts depicted on the facade have an imposing presence and are, from left to right: theater, music (with sword), literature, and poetry. The mass of the building—a large cube—is relieved by artfully placed recessions and projections. Inside the old auditorium hall, which takes up most of the central body of the building, is in disrepair and there are rumors that it may be headed for the wreckers ball or the renovator's drafting table at least. One particularly lovely detail can be found on the northern side, facing DAAP, in a split pediment doorway that Fechheimer treated with a subtle and deft hand.

8. College of Design, Architecture, Art, and Planning (DAAP)

Alms Building *George Roth & James E. Allen, 1952*
DAAP *James E. Allen, 1958*
Wolfson Hall *Tweddel Wheeler Strickland Beumer, 1976*
Aronoff Center for Design and Art
    Peter Eisenman in association with Lorenz and Williams, 1996

In 1989, the University of Cincinnati set out to redefine itself through what it called the "the signature architect program." The idea was to hire world-renowned architects to transform the campus from an at best mundane architectural setting into a place that would become an important stop on a pilgrimage to the world's great architecture. Step one in this plan, fittingly, was the design of a new home for the College of Design, Architecture, Art, and Planning, or DAAP. The commission was unusual; the architect would have to work with three existing buildings of varied architectural style, while at the same time create a statement of his or her own that would make a mark internationally. Jay Chatterjee, the dean of the architecture school, proposed the idea of mounting an invitation-only competition—at that time unheard of at the campus—in order to attract the very top architects and cull their ideas. Chatterjee's "competition" was really an invitation to a select group of notable architects to present their firms before a selection commit-tee. The list included Frank Gehry, Michael Graves, Cesar Pelli, Charles Gwathmey, Elisabeth Plater-Zyberk, Peter Eisenman, and several others; and

DAAP

College of Design, Architecture, Art, and Planning (DAAP)

DAAP, interior court

as is typically the case, the presentations were mainly slide shows in which each architect displayed its work. Except Eisenman. Unlike the others, although well-known and respected, Eisenman had little built work to show. And instead of fudging it, he turned off the slide projector and simply talked about his philosophy of architecture. The panel was taken off guard, and before long absolutely beguiled by this self-styled deconstructionist and his unconventional approach to architecture. What he talked about was his conception of architecture (based loosely on the writings of French deconstructionists) and how he would attempt to create a conceptually rich and idea-driven building to challenge architectural thinkers, of which there should be no shortage, he reasoned, in an architecture school. This was exactly what was wanted—something out of the ordinary and unexpected. Eisenman was hired.

The existing conglomeration of buildings was built between 1950 and 1976. The two oldest, the Alms Building and the original DAAP building, were designed by local architect James E. Allen in a handsome modern style. Clad in brick, the buildings are well proportioned and geometric, the horizontal rooflines and cornices reminding one of the early modernists and the paintings of Piet Mondrian. The 1976 Wolfson Hall was designed by Richard Wheeler of the local firm Tweddel Wheeler Strickland Beumer in the Brutalist manner, derided for its inhospitable interiors and inelegant appearance. The building was dedicated to Erwin S. Wolfson, an alumnus and New York developer. Eisenman's building, formally called the Aronoff Center for Design and Art after an Ohio state senator but referred to on campus as DAAP, acts as a link between these three older buildings; at its core is a corridor that runs along the perimeter of the old buildings. But architecturally it is a vastly complex corridor, one that interprets the architectural presence of the existing buildings, magnifies it, and then extrapolates it into what critics have called an entirely new form of architecture. One might call it deconstructed architecture were this appellation not so loaded with other meaning.

Eisenman used the strange conjunction of Alms, the old DAAP, and Wolfson—where they came together on their north faces—as his starting point. In a series of working drawings the jagged shape formed by the buildings, which he refers to as a chevron (as in the logo of the oil company of the same name) was inscribed and re-inscribed as if repeating itself outward from the building. Already an essentially complex shape, the chevron was then shifted on its various axes to produce a multitude of shapes, creating at this early stage what architects call a *parti,* a basic scheme or

LEFT: *DAAP, interior*
RIGHT: *DAAP, student center*

concept. After interpreting and magnifying the chevron *parti* on paper, Eisenman then translated it into three dimensions to design the building. The result is a complex geometrical assemblage that crawls down the slope from Clifton Avenue, hugging the backside of the original DAAP complex.

Within the building, Eisenman was able to convey this sense of descending and shifting with the shape of the chevron quite beautifully. The core corridor is open, but carved on all sides by walls meeting at odd angles. Along the outer edge of the building are office spaces, a library, and on the top floor studios for planning students. At the far eastern end lie two auditoriums, designed with an upper balcony accessible to the top hallway so that students can drop in for a few minutes of a lecture and leave without disturbing the proceedings—a touch imported from the auditorium at Harvard's Graduate School of Design. The central annex, beside the corridor, contains a lower level cafe where students are treated to a video installation by Nam June Paik, part of the university's growing collection of public art. This whole inner space is open to views, although there is no one place where one can grasp the whole. Rather you are pulled through by the ever-shifting geometries, which are emphasized by continuously alternating color schemes of pastel greens, pinks, and blues. Eisenman designed the building, from soup to nuts, on the computer at a time when full computer-aided design was just being developed. As a result, the design superseded reality, delaying construction as contractors struggled with how to make sure the lines that met up on the computer would actually meet up in space. A special laser transit was developed to ensure the surveying, but this and other complications delayed the actual construction for many years.

Aronoff Center for Design and Art

Because no two angles are the same, the interior space lacks equilibrium—one seems to be teetering on the edge of a non-Euclidean world that defies the traditional ordering processes of architecture. Critic Joseph Giovannini remarked that the DAAP creates "a polyvalent space without center or dominant direction." For him it was the most democratic of architectures: able to be interpreted differently by each viewer.

Most people interpret buildings from the outside, and the best place to view the Aronoff Center for Design and Art is from the northern side, along Martin Luther King Drive. From here the building looks like cascading slabs almost on the verge of slipping off—an overt sleight of hand on the part of Eisenman to make the architecture look "de-constructed." From the west, the building is sunken into grade—at the direction of the university president Joseph Steger, who worried that the building would dominate the corner where most of the visitors to the campus arrive by car. Along the north edge of the building, emerging from the slope of the grade are several landforms crafted by the landscape architect George Hargreaves, which provide a curvilinear counterpoint to Eisenman's rectilinear building.

Eisenman is the first to admit—partially because of the mandate to resist making a monumental statement on this visible corner—that the exterior of the building is not as exciting as the interior. For him the heart of the building lies in the chevronesque central corridor, or atrium, which provides a living room for the college. Here students are given a place to hang out, and many studios conduct their regular "crits" of work right here in the open. It's all part of the idea that at an architecture school, the architecture itself should inspire students.

Main Street and Athletic Complex

Clifton Avenue

McMic
Comm

9b

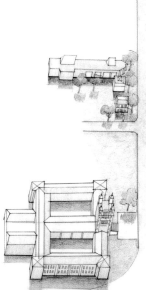

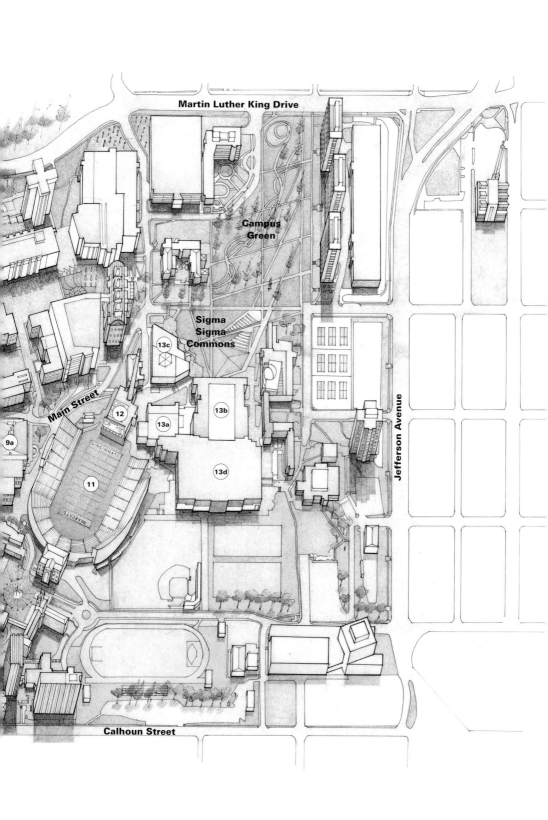

Martin Luther King Drive

Campus
Green

Sigma
Sigma
Commons

13c

Main Street

12

13a

13b

9a

11

13d

Jefferson Avenue

Calhoun Street

The Hargreaves Master Plan

We start this walk in McMicken Commons, immediately behind McMicken Hall, where the architectural ghosts of the past and harbingers of the future vie for our attention. Several old brick buildings used to reside in the middle of the commons—including "Old Tech," one of the first science buildings on campus, and Tanners, originally built by the Tanners Council of the United States. Along the edge of the green once lived Beecher Hall, the first building for women on campus, erected in 1916, but which eventually became too expensive to modernize. Beecher, built in traditional red brick with a vaguely Georgian facade and bright white limestone trim, was an all purpose "women's building," with a natatorium, gymnasium, and classrooms for the College of Education and Home Economics. Each of these is now gone, removed originally in order to create this commons, one of the first green spaces on campus proposed by the master planner and landscape architect George Hargreaves. Hargreaves designed the actual commons simply, as a system of radiating walks that tie the architectural spaces together. Most of these spaces are still on the boards, as architects say, but by closing our eyes we can imagine, in some manner, how things might look in three, four, and five years. The ultimate completion date is set for 2005.

The first change, already underway at press time, is the erection of the Center for Enrollment Services, which replaces Beecher Hall and encloses the southern edge of the commons. Directly across from McMicken Hall the student union, known as the Tangeman University Center, will be completely redesigned. Much of the structure will be removed, except the iconic tower and west- or commons-facing facade. These will be encapsulated in an airy, glass structure designed by the New York architect Charles Gwathmey. The biggest change will take place alongside this structure—where Hargreaves has designed a new "main street," which will be flanked by the Gwathmey building on one side, a new student activities on the other, and a new student recreation building farther along, down the hill. Each of these is in various stages of design, and over the next few years will enter construction, entirely disrupting this central spine of the campus. While the construction fencing and barriers are up, visitors are left to imagine what is to come.

As we descend off the ridge onto the central plain of campus, we enter the athletic complex of fields, fieldhouses, and stadium. Athletics have been a central part of life at the University of Cincinnati since the early days of the university, when young UC men would gather in the depression behind McMicken Hall and play football in the muddy river bottoms. Since then the "Bearcats" have ritually excelled at basketball and remained competitive in other Division I sports. Architecturally, the importance placed on sports is signified by the fact that the athletic complex of fields and stadia are situated in the heart of campus, rather than on the outskirts as is the case on most campuses. Architects over the last hundred years have been challenged to come up with a way to make these spaces a part of the campus as a whole. Although the idea of removing the athletics out to the perimeter of campus has been floated once or twice, there's a sense at UC that to do so would dishonor the past as much as disrupt the future. The football stadium lies in the absolute heart of the campus, in the gully where a stream once ran, and forms a visible center to academic life. Often one must walk through the stadium in order to get somewhere else, meaning that the place is always open and populated by students. Partly this is because until lately, this was the only open, green space on campus (notwithstanding the artificial turf).

The one change that will take place in the athletic center is the removal of the tennis courts from their current position to a parking lot between the Edwards Center and Daniels Hall, to create a line of fields that extends north from the stadium—a clearer precinct.

Behind the stadium is one of several generator plants on campus, a groaning, coughing presence that various architects have added to or tried to hide. In the center of the complex is a quite handsome stack, which rises elegantly above the fray. The plant has been an issue of debate for decades, with even one proposal in the 1960s to replace it with a nuclear power plant to be sunk beneath the stadium. The new power plant built on the hill between the east and west campuses (see Walk Five) has made this plant redundant, and soon it will be all but dismantled to make way for the new student recreation facility designed by architect Thom Mayne and his firm Morphosis. Original plans, however, show the stack retained as an architectural icon in the new building.

While sports fans will want to linger in Shoemaker Center where the dynastic basketball team plays, the highlight of this architectural Walk remains on the boards, as architects like to say. I've accorded the same kind of attention to the Main Street project and the four buildings that define it because, like the other major buildings in this guide, it presages the future architectural grandeur of the university. However, because it is under construction, the descriptions are all made with the disclaimer that certain changes—many minor, but certainly others quite major—will be made in the coming years, perhaps impacting the overall look of the campus quite a bit. We can only suppose what the final outcome will be.

Tangeman University Center and Tanners Lab, right

9. Tangeman University Center and Tanners Lab

Harry Hake, 1937 and 1924

The student union was built in 1937 to a design by Harry Hake, a prominent Cincinnati architect whose firm had already completed several buildings on campus. Hake, responding to the presence of Baldwin Quad and other neo-Georgian structures on campus, designed the building in the image of Independence Hall in Philadelphia, with a bare brick mast, octagonal and square stages of the tower, and an understated expressiveness that epitomized Colonial architecture. In 1937 it was meant as a patriotic statement, a veering away from the European-inspired Beaux Arts style of Van Wormer Library (now the Administration Building) and the Blegen Library. Although Hake is credited with the design, the building was erected by the Works Progress Administration, which usually commissioned several local architects when embarking on projects like this in order to spread the federal dollars around. In 1967 the union was dedicated to the memory of Donald Core Tangeman, a young navy sailor who was killed in the South Pacific during World War II and whose parents were UC alumni and longtime benefactors. Inside, despite the dark and depressing halls, are located several Rookwood fountains, designed by the renowned Cincinnati pottery firm. As part of the Main Street project (see below), Tangeman is to be gutted, stripped, and partially dismantled by the New York firm of Gwathmey Siegel. Tangeman, as it stands, wraps around a smaller more strictly Georgian structure called Tanners, or Tanning Laboratory. Originally called

Tangeman University Center

the Leather Research Building, it was also designed by Harry Hake, in 1924, about thirteen years prior to Tangeman, at which time it was intended to join several other buildings on the McMicken Common to create a quad-like precinct although the space was to be more cluttered than an ideal Beaux Arts quad. The Tanners Council of America sponsored the building as a move to inject the rigors of science into the craft of leather tanning. The structure, also adorned inside with works from Rookwood Pottery, housed chemistry classes and, for a while, a tanning institute within the college of engineering. It was also used by the early co-operative curricula programs, which were first theorized at the university by Herman Schneider, former dean of the engineering school. Today it sits derelict, awaiting, along with much of Tangeman itself, destruction. When gone, Tanners' footprint will provide McMicken Commons with the balance of open space it desperately desires as well creating, finally, a much more traditional quad setting.

10. Main Street Commons

Center for Enrollment Services

Leers Weinzapfel associated with Gartner, Burdick, Bauer-Nilson Architects 2002

Tangeman University Center

Gwathmey Siegel associated with Gartner, Burdick, Bauer-Nilson Architects, 2005

Student Recreation Center *Morphosis, 2005*

Student Life Building *Moore Ruble Yudell, 2005*

Center for Enrollment Services

The Main Street proposal is a key element of the master plan and has been on the boards for a long time. The idea, according to master planner George Hargreaves, is to create a vibrant urban center to the campus, to which students will gravitate when not in class. The buildings are all programmed with student services, food services, and general student activities centers, and the design is meant to focus energy rather than disperse it.

The core of the plan is a "main street," which curves as it descends down the hill toward the stadium. The street itself will be open to pedestrians only and designed as a narrow walkway flanked by nodes for sitting and dining along its length. Hargreaves' intention is to create a density that is in tune. Partly this is achieved by the architecture, which encroaches on each side. But beyond that Hargreaves also plans to craft the landscape as a series of plazas lining a central promenade—structurally a very traditional urban (and European) notion, to which he will undoubtedly give his own distinct, sculptural spin.

The Street sweeps through the heart of campus, from the austere commons behind McMicken down into the ravine around the Engineering Research Building, where it connects with Sigma Sigma Commons, which then leads into the Campus Green—thus forming a green spine that weaves through campus like a river. At the head of the street, providing a new edge to McMicken Commons, is the new Center for Enrollment Services, which will house the registrar, parking permits office, and other first-day-of-school offices in a single location. It is designed by Boston-based Andrea Leers and Jane Weinzapfel. The structure will rise silently in six horizontal, glass shelves to create a "window" over the commons. On the top floor a loggia will wrap around the north face. The simple rectangular form of the building establishes a connection with the so-called academic ridge of buildings on axis with McMicken Hall, as well as with the new CCM building and revamped student union (under construction on the east side of the commons). The structure will also close off the open end of the Teacher College, thus making it an actual quad. Leers and Weinzapfel, headed up by partners Jane Weinzapfel and Andrea Leers, is known mostly for tasteful, crisp, and site appropriate buildings. Perhaps the firm's best known work is a control center for the Boston transit authority, which melds gracefully with the traditional neighborhood via its classical finials and a staid stone cladding; the details, however, such as the use of perforated metal grates over the windows and the geometry of recesses in the facade, are all thoroughly contemporary and forward-looking. Here too the firm will attempt to address history and context while also presenting a sense of newness and modernity.

On the southern edge of the commons lies Tangeman University Center, which for decades has housed the student union on campus (see above). As part of the Main Street plan half of Tangeman will be taken down. Only the most important, historic components will be left—the Christopher Wren cupola and the classical facade facing McMicken Commons. These will be wrapped by a new structure designed by Gwathmey Siegel architects from New York, under the design supervision of principal Charles Gwathmey. The new student union will be an airy structure. The roof around the cupola will be penetrated by skylights to create a large, open-air atrium in the center of the building that looks out over the new Main Street to the north. While the historic facade on the commons will continue to formally greet visitors to the campus once they walk through the arch in McMicken Hall, the main center of life and activity will be along this north side, where the building steps down the hill and forms an important urban edge to the Main Street. According to architect Greg Karn, project manager for Gwathmey Siegel, a food court and movie theater will be situated along here to create a kind of open, active terrace for both the building and the street. The new wrap of the union will be thoroughly modern, constructed of zinc and glass, which will allow views to the interior structure including the old union sitting in the middle. The southern wing of Tangeman, an addition appended in the 1960s, will be entirely removed and a new wing of the new building constructed that will establish a relationship, via a skyway bridge, with the new CCM Village and Center for Enrollment Services.

Across from the new union, arching in a convex manner along the edge of the new Main Street, will be a new student life building that will house offices for all the student associations and the student government. The Santa Monica, California-based firm Moore Ruble Yudell is designing the structure as a thin, curved form that steps down the hill. The building, in

Tangeman University Center

many ways, will be the most important in the Main Street scheme, as it cre-ates the kind of torque-ing force in the curve of the street, establishing the site lines and flow of movement.

At the bottom of the hill we presently find the University Bookstore, which was designed by a consortium of architectural firms, including Ken White Associates, Design International, and Glaser Associates. Sunken into the hillside, the architecture attempts to respond to the challenging topog-raphy of the campus by creating multileveled outdoor seating areas. However, the uninspired design and the fact that the building simply sits in the way of the ambitious master plan means that its function will be removed to the new student union and the building will be torn down and replaced by the Student Recreation Center. Forming the eastern edge of the street, this large, irregularly shaped building is being designed by Thom Mayne and his Santa Monica-based firm Morphosis. The most identifiable component of the structure is a curvilinear raised spine, dubbed the "wiggle worm," which will provide townhouse-like residential units. The "wiggle worm" will compress the existing air space to create a snug, urban sensation of density. On ground level, viewed through a scrim of International Style pylons, is the low-rise recreation center that will wrap itself around the existing physical plant. The plant, which is now redundant with the new power plant on the corner of Vine Street and Martin Luther King Drive (see Walk Six), will be reduced to the bare bones of its original architecture. The stack, because of its historical and aesthetic qualities will be retained and absorbed, like an icon, into the Morphosis design. One iter-ation of the current plan has a climbing wall erected around the stack base, on the roof of the existing building—an energetic reuse that points up the eclectic nature of the campus as a whole.

As a signal of the university's ambitious approach to remaking itself, the entire Main Street project—all four buildings—is being con-structed at once. The incredible dislocation in the heart of the campus that this decision engenders has necessitated a sequence of tensile temporary structures—fancy tents, in essence—which dot opportune spaces in and around McMicken Commons and the Baldwin quad. The tents are designed by Jack Rouse Associates and Glaser Associates. To certain eyes the tents will look garish and unfortunate, but historically there's precedent. During World War II soldiers were bivouacked in front of Baldwin Hall, in the quad. Consider the construction of Main Street as a war of sorts—perhaps for UC's soul.

Nippert Stadium

11. Nippert Stadium

Garber & Woodward, 1912, 1920, 1924; James E. Allen, addition, 1954;
Baxter Hodell Donnelly & Preston, renovation, 1991

The football stadium was originally erected in 1916, and today is the sixth oldest Division I field in the country, after Harvard, Yale, Georgia Tech, Princeton, and Cornell. The spot had originally been a lagoon. It was drained and filled with excavated soil from the construction of early buildings on campus—all of which were erected on the top of the hill. From the campus beginnings the lower area immediately behind McMicken Hall was called Carson Field and used by students for games, including, as it became popular in the 1880s, American football.

In 1910 the first rise of concrete seating was constructed around the field. In 1923, during a game against rival Miami of Ohio on Thanksgiving Day, a young player named Jimmy Nippert was kicked in the leg and played the game with an open wound. A month later, he died of blood poisoning. His grandfather, James N. Gamble, donated $270,000 to complete the last ring of seating in 1924, and the stadium was dedicated to the heroic Jimmy. In the curve of the horseshoe, in front of Dieterle Hall, is a relief memorial to Nippert, sculpted by Ernest Bruce Haswell and inscribed with what were supposedly Nippert's last words: "Five more yards to go—then drop." In the 1950s James Allen, architect of the College of Design, Architecture, Art, and Planning, slightly expanded the stadium.

By the mid-1980s the old stadium needed a major renovation. Staircases, railings, seats—all were in pretty sad shape. Even more pressing were the foundation cracks, circulation bottlenecks, and various fire and safety design issues that hadn't been addressed in many decades. Many assumed, given the status of sports at UC, that the small, old stadium would be razed and a fancy, much larger one erected elsewhere. But because sports have been such an important part of the university throughout its history, the general consensus was to save the historic stadium. The planning committee looked for examples of such historic preservation and found one at Harvard, which had gone to great lengths to renovate its football stadium years before. The committee went so far as to hire the same architectural firm that did that work, Baxter Hodell Donnelly & Preston, to come out to Cincinnati and work their magic here.

The renovations, by most accounts, are a resounding success; because the work blends so seamlessly into the existing context of the stadium, it is typically overlooked in discussions of the campus' architecture. The classic horseshoe form of the stadium was retained. Additional seating for about 9,000 people was added, while a three-tier press box—critical to establishing the university as a presence in college football—was appended to the upper eastern edge. Other modernization touches included new lighting and a renovated playing surface. An enormous scoreboard was placed at the northern end, in part to hide the physical plant, but one wonders whether the garish can ever best the humdrum industrial. After two seasons of sharing Riverfront Stadium in downtown Cincinnati with the professional sports teams in town, the Bearcats returned to gleaming new Nippert as though it had dropped from heaven in 1991.

12. Utilities Plant

Garber & Woodward and Teiteg & Lee, 1910; Harry Hake and Sons, addition, 1964; Herbert Hilmer, addition, 1967

The plant was built in 1910 to supply the buildings upon the academic ridge with coal-heat and electricity. The University commissioned the Cincinnati architectural firms of Garber & Woodward and Teiteg & Lee, both of whom were then working on designs for Baldwin Hall, to design the structure. The striking stack dates to this original design, as does the inner core of the plant. In 1964 the university hired Hake and Hake, the firm of Harry Hake, the architect of McMicken Hall, to expand the plant to meet the modern West Campus's power needs. Three years later Herbert Hilmer, fresh from the completion of the Marx Library at the College of Law, was pulled in to endeavor yet another addition, along with his partner at the time, William P. Fosdick, a graduate of the Engineering College. Each of these additions was thoroughly modern in its conception. Although its founder had executed an eloquent

Utilities Plant

mid-century evocation of Georgian architectural style at McMicken Hall, the Harry Hake firm, by the mid-1960s, was steeped in the sensibilities of the time. The 1964 design wrapped the old brick plant in a jumble of steel-caged canisters, piping, groaning mini-stacks, and steam-huffing vents. By the time all of these additions were completed the power plant was a loud, guffawing annoyance in the heart of campus—necessary but rude.

13. Athletic Complex

Laurence Hall *James E. Allen, 1961*
Armory Fieldhouse *James E. Allen, 1955*
University Bookstore
    Ken White Associates/Design International/Glaser & Associates, 1981
Myrl H. Shoemaker Center *Glaser & Associates, 1989*

The sequence of buildings and fields that wrap around Nippert Stadium comprises the athletic complex in the heart of campus. The fields, in some manner, have occupied these sites for half a century or longer; but in recent years the university has invested in modernizing them with new drainage, resilient surfacing, and other redesigns.

The complex of buildings houses both varsity sports and general recreational facilities for the university. The Fieldhouse was originally used for drilling soldiers for preparedness during the height of the Cold War. It has been used for various varsity sports and intramural athletics since then, undergoing a $200,000

TOP: *Myrl H. Shoemaker Center*
BOTTOM: *Armory Fieldhouse*

TOP: *University Bookstore*
BOTTOM: *The "Big O"*

renovation in the late 1980s. But the center is now outdated, and many of the intramural and fitness activities will be moved to the new student recreational center that is being built as part of the Main Street project (see above).

The Myrl H. Shoemaker Center was erected in 1989 to a design by local Cincinnati architects Glaser & Associates, and is symbolic of the university's continued dominance in the sport of basketball. Although the structure dominates, as well, the landscape of the campus, it has been lauded for its interior design, which includes seating for 13,000, private suites for VIPs, and extensive weight training and sports medicine facilities. The center was constructed at a time when the basketball team was in a slump and the athletic director was hoping to rekindle a bygone era of greatness. At $25 million, the center illustrates how important such hopes are to Division I schools with banner sports programs. With the seats packed for almost every game, it has become a kind of de facto public forum for the students. Since the construction of the center in 1989, the Bearcats basketball team has once again ascended to the top ranks. On the eastern face of the building, in front of the main entrance, stands a statue of the most famous alumnus of the team, Oscar Robertson, cast in bronze by sculptor Blair Buswell. Known as the "Big O," Robertson here seems larger than life, right down to his Converses. With his career record at Cincinnati of 79-7 inscribed on the plinth, perhaps larger than life is appropriate.

The Center was named after Myrl Shoemaker, for many years the university's protector in the Ohio legislature.

Baldwin Quad and

Engineering Research Center

Clifton Avenue

McMicken
Commons

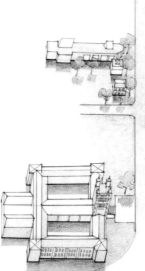

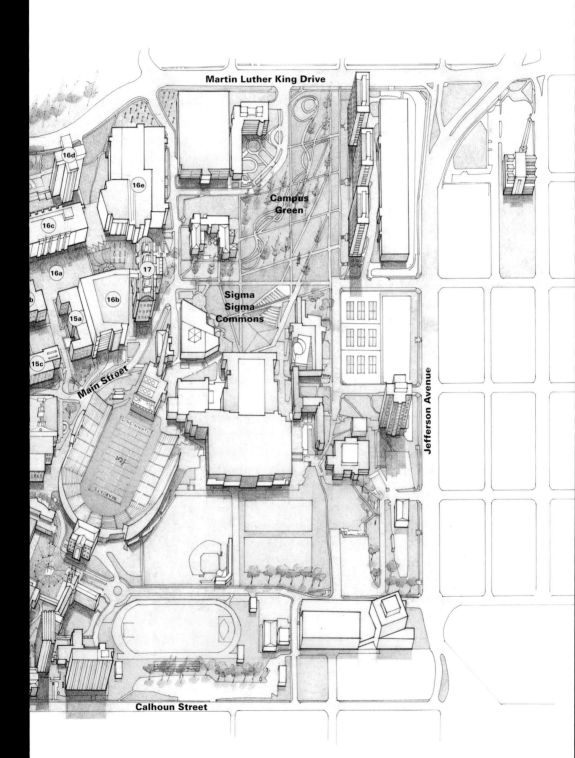

Martin Luther King Drive

Campus
Green

16d

16e

16c

16a

17

16b

15a

16b

15c

Sigma
Sigma
Commons

Main Street

CINCINNATI

Jefferson Avenue

Calhoun Street

In 1910, the university branched out from its academic ridge along Clifton Avenue and began development of three new buildings, to form an open quadrangle. At the time, this was a very popular planning scheme for American universities, an academic parallel to the City Beautiful movement inspired by the French Beaux-Arts tradition and embraced by a generation of American architects and planners. The Baldwin Quad, so-named for the building at the apex of the quadrangle, is currently entering a period of transition, during which the interiors of several of the buildings are being redesigned and modernized. At the same moment, the open space in the middle of the quad will be occupied for several years by a semi-permanent tent that will house various dislocated university offices while the Main Street project is underway. Nonetheless, it is possible to poke around the edges of this kerfuffle and get a sense of the intimate, classically laid out green between the buildings. After the Main Street project is completed the university plans to renovate the green; landscape architect George Hargreaves has already started on conceptual renderings that show a general greening up of the area.

The entire complex of buildings around Library Square, encompassing Rhodes Hall, Zimmer Auditorium, Rieveschl Hall and Crosley Tower, was all once known as the Brodie Science Complex—a change indicative of how campus architecture has become stuffed full of significant names and laden with all sorts of dedicatory appellations. Today, because of the unmistakable presence of Michael Graves' Engineering Research Center, most everyone refers to the area as the ERC. Between the buildings, acting as a magnet that gives them focus and purpose, is a new square designed by George Hargreaves—dubbed Library Square. The space epitomizes one key aspect of the master plan, which is to create a sequence of small plazas between buildings where students can congregate. The concept is essentially that of the classical forum: a place that will stimulate and support public dialogue, no matter how rancorous. And yet it is done here in a particularly modern way. The architecture actually gives rise to the landscape: molding, cupping, and shaping it. In response, Hargreaves' design is thoroughly urban—a paved plaza with architectonic sculptural forms—to convey the idea that this is not a place for quiet meditation, but rather for interaction with others.

With the exception of the ERC itself, the buildings that surround Library Square and comprise this precinct were all constructed in 1969 and 1970 during a building boom. Although at the time fulfilling a dire need for space, today the whole lot is almost universally despised on campus as inhospitable, cold, and frankly unattractive. The capstone is Crosley Tower, which dominates the ERC area and can be seen from almost anywhere on campus.

As one can imagine looking upon its massive concrete form, very little light penetrates the tower, making it seem unlivable to the poor souls entombed within. As has been the case with unsightly towers in the past, the university is considering demolishing and replacing it with something more in harmony with the master plan. Perhaps the best building in the lot, and one that probably shouldn't be lumped in with the rest, is the Langsam Library. While the other buildings display their bulk ostentatiously, like an architectural version of professional wrestling, the Langsam Library tries to reduce its presence in a classically modernist way, with roof overhangs and a flat, horizontal presence—all the while achieving the impressive feat of housing the university's large general collection.

The masterpiece in this walk is the ERC, designed by Michael Graves and erected in 1992. Graves attended UC's architecture school as an undergraduate before moving on to Princeton for graduate school—where he now practices. As a favored alum he was included in the first competition of the signature architect program, that for the design of the DAAP (see Walk One). When that commission went to Peter Eisenman instead, dean Jay Chatterjee advised Graves to try again, this time for the ERC commission. The way it all played out was fortuitous. Graves' approach is much more monumental than Eisenman's, and his talents are far more appropriate for this conspicuous site than off in the corner where the DAAP resides. Despite this monumentality, however, the ERC is a graceful building that conforms very neatly with the master plan by forming an edge to Library Square on one side and the Campus Green on the other, two landscapes of vastly different scales and aesthetic, which the building seems to bridge effortlessly.

14. Braunstein Hall and Geology and Physics

Braunstein Hall *Crowe & Schulte, 1933; Cyrus Baxter, addition, 1948*
Geology and Physics *E. A. Glendening, 1987*

Braunstein Hall was built originally to hold the physics department in the College of Engineering. It was designed by prominent Cincinnati architect Edward Schulte—whose firm, Crowe & Schulte, was the leading Catholic firm in the city at the time and responsible for most of the churches in the archdiocese. Schulte was a brash young man who, after working for a succession of firms in the city including that of Harry Hake, set out on his own with business partner Robert Crowe. Schulte understood traditional American architecture and designed Braunstein partly in the Colonial or Georgian style to conform to nearby Baldwin Quad, with hints of

Geology and Physics

neo-Gothic (then quite in vogue on academic campuses)—such as the tall arched windows and extensive limestone trim. There are also modern, almost Art Deco, details in the structure that shouldn't go unnoticed, such as patterning of the bricks, which get wider and shorter higher up, and the almost Moorish-looking sculptural motif of the larger circle enclosing a smaller circle. Structurally, the building was constructed in steel and concrete with a brick curtain wall. The angular addition to the building off the east wing was designed by Cincinnati architect Cyrus Baxter in 1948 and is a sensitive accouterment to the original design.

Immediately behind Braunstein Hall is the squat, modernistic Geology and Physics building. Although the grade slopes off behind Braunstein, architect E. A. Glendening chose to ignore this and instead retain the same roofline as Braunstein, causing the building, in effect, to soar. To reduce the massing of the building the ground floor is much smaller than the overhanging upper floors, creating a dark, shaded plaza between it and Braunstein. The use of red brick is an overt attempt to connect, aesthetically, with an architectural tradition on campus.

15. Baldwin Quad

Baldwin Hall *Teitig & Lee and Garber & Woodward, 1911*
Old Chemistry *Teiteg & Lee, 1917; Harry Hake, addition, 1938*
Swift Hall *Harry Hake, 1925*

The Baldwin Quad represents the second phase of the university's development, as it outgrew the strict linear formation of buildings that climbed up the ridge along Clifton Avenue and branched out eastward along a more traditional quadrangle design. The "quad" by the 1920s had become ubiquitous on American campuses. Like the Jeffersonian "village," the quad—usually left open-ended—created a central green between buildings that symbolized the social and democratic heart of the educational institution. It was also the form favored by the École de Beaux Arts in Paris, the most influential force in American architecture at the beginning of the twentieth century. The Baldwin Quad was actually formed over a period of fourteen years, from the completion of Baldwin Hall on the eastern end in 1911 to the completion of Swift Hall on the southern edge in 1925. Strangely, the quad didn't follow the geometry already established on campus. Instead it was sited off Clifton Avenue and the line of buildings along Clifton's length at an angle of thirteen degrees, thus introducing—as would later be recognized by the 1990s master plan and signature buildings—a new "force field" of orientation on the campus (see Introduction).

Baldwin Hall was designed by two prominent Cincinnati firms, Teiteg & Lee and Garber & Woodward. Both firms were known for their Beaux Arts vocabulary and their work in traditional styles. Frederick Garber and his partner Clifford Woodward attended Massachusetts Institute of Technology, as did Teiteg, and all were versed in the Colonial or Georgian style of architecture. Teiteg and his partner Walter Lee also designed several houses in the Arts and Crafts style, and thus were also cognizant of some of the early modernizing influences on traditional architecture. Baldwin Hall and her sister structures display the effect of all these facts—a tender looking backward to the past, an understanding of Colonial and indeed patriotic architecture and its derivations, and a few modernizations or streamlining features that point toward emerging sensibilities. The main structure, Baldwin Hall, is laid out as a simple rectangular building, flanked at each end by smaller wings. The portico features a classical pediment limned with excessive filigree. Enormous fluted Ionic columns tower in front. The moldings that run the length of the building, the detail around the windows, and the even division of the mass into stories all hint at the modernizing influences entering architectural practice at this time.

Both Swift Hall and Old Chemistry, which were built later, are streamlined and calm companions to Baldwin. Old Chemistry, designed by Teiteg & Lee, shows an Arts and Crafts influence. The pediments are all

TOP: *Baldwin Hall*
BOTTOM: *Old Chemistry*

Swift Hall

unadorned stone. The facade is divided into even stories with a pure spacing of windows. The horizontal geometry is emphasized by the simple dentilling running the length of the building, including the very delicate touch of copper capping running along the rooftop. Note the decorative touches of an early UC coat of arms about the door, almost Art Deco in inspiration. Swift, designed by Harry Hake in 1925, is a replica of Old Chemistry with an even simpler arrangement of the facade, lacking almost all decoration. The two structures offer complementary pedagogical advice in the slogans carved into their facades: "Knowledge and Experience" on Swift and "Theory and Practice" on Old Chem. Inside Old Chem we find a famous Rookwood Pottery fountain adorned with classical science iconography. The seven symbols across the top are from Chaldean symbolism and refer at once to a planet and primary metal (from left to right): the sun and gold, Venus and copper, Mars and iron, Jupiter and tin, Saturn and lead, the moon and silver, and Mercury and mercury. The large panel in the middle of the fountain depicts a medieval soda plant.

Taken together the three buildings originally comprised what was called the Schneider Quad, so named for Herman Schneider, a dean of the College of Engineering who developed the first "co-op" curriculum. A small semicircular seating area—or exedra as it's known architecturally—commemorating Schneider anchors the open end of the green, opposite Baldwin Hall. The green will be used for a tensile tent structure to house dining facilities until the buildings along the new "main street" are completed in 2005.

16. Library Square

Zimmer Hall *Glaser, Myers & Associates, 1970*
Rhodes Hall *Baxter Hodell Donnelly & Preston, 1970*
Rieveschl Hall *A.M. Kinney, 1969*
Crosley Tower *A.M. Kinney, 1969*
Langsam Library *Glaser, Myers & Associates, 1970*
Library Square *George Hargreaves and Wes Jones, 1997*

Library Square was designed in 1997 to unify this precinct of buildings.
Landscape architect and university master planner George Hargreaves
conceived of the space as distinctly urban: small, intimate, and public. The
intent is to create a space for students to congregate, in the belief (articulated throughout the master plan) that just as much or more learning takes
place outside the classroom as within. Weight restrictions for an underground parking garage beneath the site prohibited the planting of trees. In
light of this, Hargreaves used paving to create an open plaza. The design of
the ground plane is in the shape of a nautilus, a symbol ripe with signifi-
cance in academe. Most specifically it refers to the ever-spiraling sequence
described by the Italian mathematician Fibonnaci, which ever since ancient
times has been thought to express the perfect symmetry of nature. In the
center of the form, in diminutive type, is a beguiling quote attributed to
Oliver Wendell Holmes. To compensate for the lack of verticality—which
would have been provided by trees in the plaza—Hargreaves designed a
grid of slender neon triangles, each about five feet tall, that are illuminated
at night. From above, the grid contrasts with the organic form of the nautilus, while at ground level it breaks up the monotony of the space. On the
eastern end of the plaza, connecting to another rooftop plaza sorely in
need of renovation, rests a purple staircase designed by architect Wes
Jones. Jones used a confection of materials, including glass, steel grates,
and kindergarten-colored steel supports, to devise an eye-catching scheme
that, unfortunately, hasn't weathered very well outdoors.

The building that the Jones staircase surmounts is called Zimmer Hall
and houses the largest auditorium on campus. It was designed in 1970 by the
local powerhouse firm of Glaser, Myers & Associates. Although appearing
quite dated, the interior contains a lush composition of geometric patterns,
especially in the maddeningly Escher-like extruded brick inner wall around the
auditorium. The building is set into the grade, providing a transition between
Baldwin Quad uphill and Library Square downhill. Immediately adjacent to
Zimmer is Rhodes Hall, also designed in 1970 by the Cincinnati firm of Baxter
Hodell Donnelly & Preston, which is still working on commissions on campus
today. It was named for former governor of the state, James A. Rhodes. It features a similar exterior composition of concrete buttresses, glass curtain wall,
and textured concrete cornice. It also makes a nod across the square to

LEFT: *Rieveschl Hall and Langsam Library*
RIGHT: *Langsam Library and Library Square*

Langsam Library with the horizontal composition of its upper floors, intended
in part to reduce the massive sense of the building. On the other side of
Zimmer sits Rieveschl Hall, named after professor of chemistry George
Rieveschl, developer of the antihistamine known by its commercial brand
name, Benadryl. The hall, along with Crosley Tower behind it, is formed by
massive concrete buttresses or columns that flare at the top like the hands of a
supplicant. For the time being Crosley Tower is a symbol of UC. It rises
strangely on the horizon from most viewpoints around campus, creating—to
the chagrin of many—a visual signpost. The tower is also a totem of the 1970s,
when the university was in the business of erecting tall, stand-alone towers—
supposedly in order to house students and academic departments more effectively, but also, one suspects, to convey a message that the university, like the
great cities in the world, was sophisticated, worldly, and urbane—characteris-
tics, in the 1970s, that were communicated by tall buildings. Local firm A.M.
Kinney Associates also designed this building as a square, fluted pylon that
rises into the sky. Cast in concrete, the hefty central flutes on each side flair at
the top in abstracted Corinthian fashion just like Rieveschl Hall, but here they
contain ventilation shafts for the chemistry labs within. According to some, the
reason for tearing down the tower is found in the relative rapidity of the original concrete pour, which thirty years later has begun to compromise the structural integrity of the building, although it is safe. The style of both buildings is
Brutalist, an architecture born after World War II, when materials and architects
were in short supply, and mass housing, largely outside of Paris and in Britain,
was done on the cheap with simple unadorned concrete—*concrete brute* in
French. Theoretically, the Brutalist buildings were more "honest." They lacked
the veneer that, architects like Le Corbusier argued, fooled the eye by covering
up the building. But over time the style assumed as much stylization and
adornment as the traditional architectural styles it criticized. Both Rieveschl Hall
and Crosley Tower feature visually powerful stylizations along their rooflines,
perhaps innovative at the time but now considered by most at UC as garish.

The last building on the square is Langsam Library, named for Walter
Langsam, president of the college during 1955–1971. The siting of the building

TOP: *Rhodes and Baldwin Halls*
BOTTOM: *Crosley Tower*

in the late 1960s was a point of contention. During the discussions, one idea called for razing old Nippert Stadium, which many thought would be less of an intrusion located at the perimeter of campus, in order to build a library in its place. The advantages were obvious—the library would lie in the heart of campus, a symbol of the flow of information much like blood in a body. But sports are almost as important to the university (some would say more important), and the proposal created so much outrage it was dropped. The preferred site, chosen by Texas planning consultants Candill Rowlett & Scott, located the building in the growing engineering area, along its northern edge, effectively creating a quad. The design, developed by the Cincinnati architectural firm of Glaser, Myers & Associates, embraced a variant on Prairie Style modernism. Detailing such as the dark brick and the steel trim, the windows cut into the structure like geometric relief drew on the existing Rieveschl Hall, Zimmer Auditorium, and Rhodes Hall across the plaza. The library was hailed at the time for its vast expansion of the university's holdings (from tens of thousands to over a million) and its information technology system. The interiors feature large, overhanging masses of concrete, which give the sensation of being inside a vast concrete diamond. From the outside the building is sensitive to the site and cascades down the hill to the north.

17. Engineering Research Center

Michael Graves in association with KZF Incorporated, 1992

The Engineering Research Center is the signature building on campus most obviously steeped in the tradition of college architecture. Although thoroughly original, the building features detailing that exudes an almost historic character. The doors are all heavy, the railings and wood trim are handsomely crafted and joined, and every detail of the design seems to speak of a slow, careful construction. Materially speaking, it is the exact opposite of Peter Eisenman's DAAP, where cheaper materials were used in order to execute a highly complex design. The composition of ERC, in contrast, is quite simple. The rectangular and strikingly narrow building (when viewed from the north or south) is composed of four bays, with one of the central bays privileged and made larger. The structure rises an impressive eight stories to create a presence on campus, especially when viewed from the west across Sigma Sigma Commons and the new Campus Green. The roofline with its collage of forms—the architect's signature use of the cylinder juxtaposed with the rectangle—catches the eye first. The dark hues are weathered copper—a material with strength and solidity, yet graceful and elegant.

Graves, who informed UC's design selection committee that he'd never done a laboratory before, worked with the laboratory specialist firm

Engineering Research Center

of Smith, Hinchman & Grylls to make sure that the needs of the engineering department for dust-free, vibration-free, and well-ventilated rooms were met, while at the same time designing a building that inside and out would be inspirational. The exterior is composed of orange terracotta Ohio sandstone. George Hargreaves also used an Ohio stone for entry markers at several of the campus gateways. Along with this there are bluestone panels and precast concrete spans between the lintels, all of which create a subtle interplay of colors and textures, heightened by the use of primary geometric forms. The building essentially has two fronts—one of which faces the Library Square, the other of which opens onto Sigma Sigma Commons. Connecting the two is a cavernous, barrel-vaulted multileveled atrium, finished in brick at a scale that bespeaks academia. It actually is sited right on axis with a major pedestrian route through campus and is intended almost like an outdoor path for transiting traffic. The staircase that descends through the middle has an almost ceremonial aspect.

Inside the building, the space is divided up into specialized labs ringed by a narrow hallway and perimeter offices. The windows, fashioned as distinctive portholes, flood the hallway with light, which then is allowed to penetrate into the inner labs through interior windows. On the top floor, overlooking Sigma Sigma Commons, is a loggia.

Originally, the dean of the engineering school wanted to place this building in the middle of Campus Green, which at the time was a vast parking lot. But this space had already been designated for a five-acre "campus

TOP: *Sigma-Sigma and Engineering Research Center*
BOTTOM: *Engineering Research Center corridor*

Engineering Research Center entrance lobby

Engineering Research Center

green" that was to act as a key connector between the West Campus and East Campus in the master plan. Almost unanimously, those involved with the master plan, from president Steger to dean Jay Chatterjee, rejected this idea. "We're not land rich," remarked university architect Ron Kull. "We have 170 acres. We're in the middle of a city. Open space and landscape are more important in terms of quality of life than buildings. And I'm serious." Thus the building was sited along the edge of this space, forming an important boundary to Library Square and setting up a kind of monumental approach from the east that is much more appropriate.

Southeast Campus and CCM Village

Clifton Avenue

McMic
Comm

J. Miles Wolf

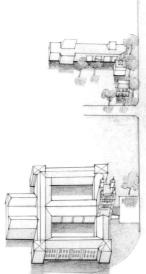

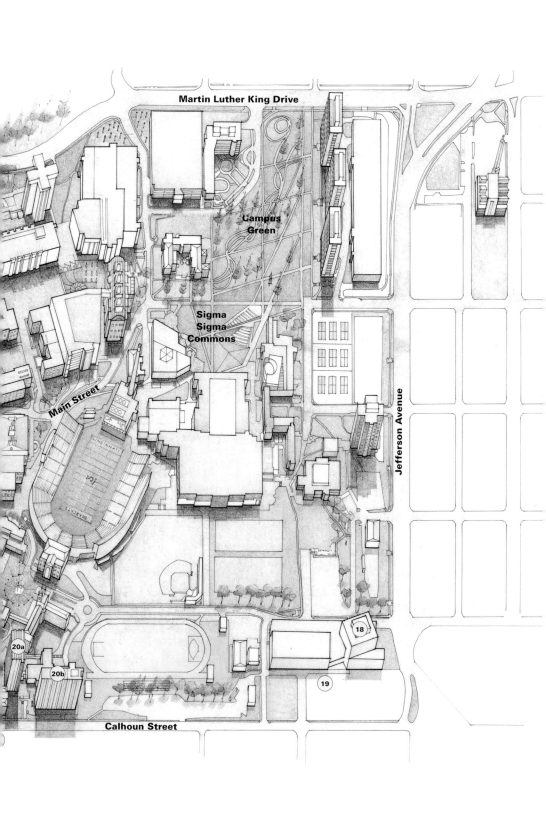

Martin Luther King Drive

Campus
Green

Sigma
Sigma
Commons

Main Street

CINCINNATI

Jefferson Avenue

20a

20b

18

19

Calhoun Street

Campus Borders

The southeast perimeter of campus borders an attractive neighborhood, referred to rather unimaginatively as Calhoun/McMillan for the streets that define it. Besides several nice shops, the neighborhood features some lovely architecture, including St. George Church and the Catholic School next door, neither of which is part of the university. Along Calhoun Street, as we walk between these buildings, you will need to imagine how the university planners, along with several neighborhood organizations, would like to spruce things up a bit—in particular, towards the top of the hill at the intersection of Calhoun Street and Jefferson Avenue, where a conceptual plan calls for removing much of the strip mall and fast food development in lieu of more densely packed, village-type development of small shops, theaters, and the like.

Along this Walk we will visit two signature buildings. The first, the Edwards Center or so-called Swing-Space Building, was designed by David Childs of the New York modernist powerhouse Skidmore Owings and Merrill. Built in 1992, it was the first new building under the master plan. While less striking than the other signature buildings, the Edwards Center does provide us—in the rotated tower on its eastern end—with one of the most forceful and obvious interpretations of the campus: a direct nod to the conflicting orientations or "force fields" that occur on the campus. The second major building is actually a complex of buildings called the College Conservatory of Music Village or CCM, designed by Henry Cobb of the New York firm Pei Cobb Freed, and completed in 2000. The college and the conservatory were originally separate schools, with the latter being the first organized in 1867 by Clara Baur, a German immigrant. The combined schools now form an internationally recognized college within UC and occupy several older buildings (Memorial Hall and the Dieterle Center) as well as several 1970s structures (Corbett Pavilion and Auditorium). All of these were unified by Henry Cobb and given an architectural center, as it were, by a long brick wing, punctuated along its roofline by distinctive pyramidal luminaires. At first glance the CCM complex doesn't seem that important. It certainly isn't as flashy as other signature buildings and resists announcing itself to the visitor. But architecturally it is a masterpiece, from the incredibly sensitive interior design to the intelligent siting decisions. More than perhaps any other building on campus (at least until the Main Street project is completed), it performs a central role in the master plan, at once connecting spaces, dividing them, and acting as both functional and beautiful architecture should.

While these two buildings are the focus of this Walk, our ramble will also take us past two of the more wonderful old buildings on campus. The first of these is Samuel Hannaford's St. George Church, which was constructed in 1873. It is a marvelous interpretation of Romanesque cathedral architecture, designed for the large German Catholic population that once lived in the neighborhood. The other is the YMCA building, designed by the local firm of Zettel and Rapp in the early 1930s. This too has Gothic overtones, though the composition relies more on the humble style of the Arts and Crafts movement. Inside we find some of the best views of campus.

18. Edwards Center

David Childs of Skidmore Owings & Merrill with Glaser Associates, 1992

The Edwards Center was the first building to be constructed as part of the 1989 master plan—yet by definition it has played a role in each subsequent move in that plan. Dubbed the "Swing-Space Building" until its dedication, the structure was built for the purpose of housing a revolving array of university departments during their dislocation as the campus tears down structures, builds anew, and generally shuffles things around. As a result of this "be anything, be everything" program, the interior of the building was left practically unfinished, so that its tenants can configure the space to their needs. One of the first inhabitants was the sprawling College of Design, Architecture, Art and Planning, which set up shop here in the early 1990s while awaiting the construction of their new home, DAAP, across campus. As part of its signature program, the design committee sought out New York architect David Childs, a partner in Skidmore Owings and Merrill, a venerable firm that got its start in 1936, a few years after the French architect Le Corbusier visited New York and shocked the American architectural scene with his revolutionary modernism. SOM, architects of the Lever House in New York, became one of the strongest voices of modernism on these shores. Since then the firm has designed literally thousands of skyscrapers, office buildings, urban plans, and airports around the world. Famously, the firm produced the Sears Tower in Chicago, for a long time the tallest building in the world. Childs ran the Washington, DC office of SOM before moving on to the New York office. He is best known for his work on the planning of Pennsylvania Avenue and the design of the Worldwide Plaza building on Manhattan's west side. Although SOM's heritage lies in the theory-laden world of early twentieth-century modernism (the time of Mies van der Rohe, early Frank Lloyd Wright, and Walter Gropius), Childs has vocally eschewed abstract principle-driven design in favor of a philosophy he calls "appropriate architecture." Basically stated, the idea is that a building should conform to sites and uses rather than to this or that aesthetic principle. The slippery slope in this, of course, is that an "appropriate" architecture might simply produce banal, uninteresting buildings.

Edwards Hall / Corry Garage

The Edwards Center, so named shortly after construction for Vera Clement Edwards, one of the first black women to earn a master's degree from and teach at UC, derives most of its power from the simple gesture of dividing the mass into unbalanced halves and twisting the upper floors of one half slightly off axis—thirteen degrees off to be exact. In effect, the building expresses the two contrasting orientations of the campus in this area: the primary, orthogonal grid of the earliest buildings constructed on the ridge and the secondary, slightly off-axis line of postwar buildings that follows the course of the ravine, of which Nippert Stadium is the strongest example. These orientations (and a third, established by Baldwin Quad on the other side of campus) are what planner George Hargreaves calls the "force fields" that have unconsciously arisen in the campus and which all future development will attempt to respect and strengthen. The Edwards Center, the first building constructed under the aegis of the master plan, serves as probably the best advertisement of how this complex scheme works. The structure also conforms neatly to the master plan by including in its design a large surface parking garage, which the office space rests upon as if on a stage. Because of the garage and the fact that land rises in this southeast corner of the campus to create a kind of rim, the Edwards Center is a highly visible building.

19. St. George Church *Samuel Hannaford, 1873*

St. George Church

St. George was built when the growing German-American population of Cincinnati was moving beyond its small community down near the river and expanding up into the heights north of the city, including the neighborhood of Corryville that bounds the eastern edge of campus. Samuel Hannaford, architect of the Music Hall and Memorial Hall downtown as well as the first McMicken Hall at the university (since replaced with the one standing), was commissioned for the design. A versatile historian of architecture, Hannaford produced an excellent approximation of a German Romanesque cathedral, with two sharp spires reaching upwards 190 feet and a single hall with delicate columns and groined vaults. The stained glass windows depicting biblical scenes were added later. The dark, expressive brick and intricate texturing of the various vertical planes of the spires recall the great Romanesque Revivalist H.H. Richardson, with whose work Hannaford was familiar. The copper roofs culminate in sparkling gold crosses, while the clock towers long stopped functioning and now read different times. Although Hannaford used a limited selection of materials—mostly brick and some stone—the interplay of surfaces, decoration, and the rhythmic massing of the building features (wing, face, tower, portico) combine to make the structure fascinatingly complex. A study of Hannaford's works in Cincinnati noted several aspects of St. George that appeared derived from the Italian Renaissance, in particular from the church of San Lorenzo in Vincenza. Both facades are organized with a large rounded-arch entry set within a gable, a series of so-called blind arches over the entrance (the windows in a line above the door), and a large imposing "wheel" window up high in the center of the facade.

In 1993, long after most of the German immigrants had moved on, the parish of St. George merged with that of St. Monica's nearby, and the future of the church was in doubt. There was talk of the university purchasing the property and tearing it down, but a preservation movement arose, amassed the funds to purchase the decaying structure, and opened the building as a quasi-religious community center. Partial renovations have been executed, but there's still more work to be done. The adjacent friary is used as office space while the small courtyard on Calhoun Street has been left to disuse.

20. Siddall and Calhoun Halls

Siddall Hall *Tweddel, Wheeler, Strickland, and Beumer, 1964*
Calhoun Hall *Tweddel, Wheeler, Strickland and Beumer, 1967*

Calhoun Hall

These matching buildings were built as dormitories to house the rapidly booming residential population of the university in the late 1960s. Both were designed by the Cincinnati firm of Tweddel, Wheeler, Strickland and Beumer, though the earlier building also saw the involvement of an early firm of Sander Hall architect Woodie Garber. Each building mixes the traditional Cincinnati brick with the International Style vocabulary of steel beams, paneling, and glass. The International Style prevails in the plain rectangular form of each building. Their architectural interest lies in how the buildings intersect and the spaces they create between them. Situated perpendicular to one another on different but related grades, the buildings create a kind of sliding geometry of rectangles both vertical and horizontal that, potentially at least, could give rise to an interesting series of pavilions and gardens. One terrace was constructed behind Calhoun, but alone and neglected it doesn't attempt to interpret the provocative geometries. The most interesting moment in either building takes place along the Calhoun Street edge, where Calhoun Hall, sunken below grade, pushes up against the street and creates an intensified, urban feeling. The vertical metal strips on both buildings were actually suggested by then president Walter Langsam, who thought that by extending them beyond the roofline the building might actually enter into a kind of architectural dialogue with the Gothic protrusions found on the adjacent Memorial Hall and YMCA building. Siddall Hall was built as a women's dormitory when female students were still housed separately from males. It was named in honor of Mrs. Kelly Y. Siddall, a presence in civic life and wife of a Procter and Gamble executive. The roof was originally designed for a sundeck, with magnificent views of downtown Cincinnati and the Ohio River.

In 1915 the University of Cincinnati contracted with the Young Men's Christian Association (YMCA) of Cincinnati to open a branch on campus. The volunteer service organization was to serve as an outlet for extracurricular activities and to address the growing role that religion was having in university life. The German American firm Zettel & Rapp designed the building in 1930; the firm was known in the city for its work on the industrial warehouses and buildings that fueled the local economy. Like Albert Kahn in Detroit and other industrial architects, Zettel & Rapp (originally known as Rapp, Zettel, & Rapp) also designed the mansions of the owners of those companies. The major design force in the firm was John Zettel, who obviously understood well the Gothic style and employed it here in order to harmonize this small house with Memorial Hall nearby (see below). The building is sunken into grade on its facade along Calhoun Street and then emerges as a much larger, three-story structure on the north, where it overlooks the campus. The interior remains well preserved, including wonderful, exposed timber beams, an airy layout, and four iron chandeliers. The most notable room is the glass-enclosed loggia overlooking campus; from here one can get a great view of campus—in particular, how the orientation of the stadium contrasts with the orientation of the buildings on the ridge (which are perpendicular to this building) and establishes one of the so-called "force fields" on campus.

The Y has operated as a kind of surrogate student center for seventy years. Since the beginning, artwork has been displayed in the large

YMCA

common room. Upstairs there are attractive meeting rooms for various organizations. From the outside, the Y presents itself as an attractive experiment in the Collegiate Gothic style that came to dominate American school architecture, especially on the East Coast.

22. College-Conservatory of Music (CCM Village)

CCM Village *Henry Cobb in association with NBBJ, 2000*
Corbett Auditorium *Edward J. Schulte, 1967*
Corbett Theater *Ming Cho Lee, 1972*
Memorial Hall *Harry Hake, 1924*
Dieterle Center *Harry Hake, 1910*

The College-Conservatory of Music, known as the CCM on campus, occupies several buildings adjacent to Nippert Stadium; under the direction of architect Henry Cobb, these were united to create a kind of "village" for the arts. Cobb, a partner in the Boston firm Pei Cobb Freed, is known for his refined, intelligent buildings and his attention to detail. His resume includes both the John Hancock Tower in Boston and that city's new federal courthouse.

Cobb's work on the CCM was three-part. First, he was charged with radically modifying two existing buildings, the Corbett Auditorium and the Corbett Pavilion. Secondly, he was to develop a new home for the school's administrative offices, several new classrooms, and a new chamber music auditorium. And lastly, he was somehow to unify the disparate assemblage of buildings, to give the college an identifiable presence. On the first part, Cobb performed a major renovation of Corbett Auditorium, originally designed by local Cincinnati architect Edward Schulte—whose other work on campus is Braunstein Hall. The frame of the original structure and the rectangular tower that houses the staging area for sets are all that remain. Cobb designed a new atrium that wraps around the concrete structure in red brick. By leaving the original exterior facing of the pavilion, he creates a dialogue between the old and new. Inside the auditorium this dialogue evolves into a one-way lecture on taste by Cobb alone. Ron Kull, the university architect who oversees all design and construction on campus, remembers the old auditorium as having Formica walls among other retrograde and unacoustical touches. Cobb's work went in other directions, partly toward the majesty of old-fashioned opera houses and partly towards the quiet meditation of a dark Boston library. (Cobb himself is a Bostonian.) The walls are finished in richly colored bubinga dowels, an African hardwood with the visual resonance of mahogany, set against a felt tapestry that captures sound and reduces echo. Large structural columns would have proved an eyesore, so Cobb designed a series of arching torchere lights with

TOP: *CCM Village (Timothy Hursley)*
BOTTOM: *Southeast entrance of CCM, off Corbett Drive (Mark Lyons)*

Corbett Auditorium

rubbed steel. Acoustical engineering firm Kirkegaard & Associates con-
sulted on the project, and you can see the firm's hand everywhere beneath
Cobb's aesthetic touches, such as the banners hanging in the ceiling.

Behind the auditorium (accessed by walking around the auditorium's
exterior toward the west), Cobb built a studio theater that one-ups a traditional
black box. If the auditorium presents itself as a variant on the European opera
house, the studio theater looks to Roman ruins for its inspiration. The walls are
blown aggregate with an internal structure of brick curved arches that, in form,
are reminiscent of Roman ruins. The space can be made into many configurations, with a gallery above to bend to the whims of set designers and directors.
Continuing our path behind the auditorium—the circular construction of which
creates the spatial structure for the interior spaces—Cobb's wrapping structure
includes an enormous staging space for set construction and a series of subter-
ranean support spaces, including a wig shop, costume shop, and prosthetics
lab (for creating Cyrano de Bergerac's nose among other things).

Appended to the far southern end of the auditorium is the Corbett
Theater, a smaller conical theater designed by Ming Cho Lee of New York.
The structure is set into the hillside, which echoes its form. Cobb left much
of this building alone, choosing instead to run a low brick wall around part
of its exterior to form a system of small courtyard gardens that wrap around
the eastern side. These were designed by landscape architect Laurie Olin,
known for his work on Bryant Park in New York. The interior theater is
smaller than the auditorium, seats 250 people, and was finished by Lee
in stunning Disco-Age decor—including a sunburst red-orange seating

Corbett Auditorium (Scott Francis)

Corbett Recital Hall

pattern. Both the auditorium and pavilion were named for donors Patricia and J. Ralph Corbett, the latter being the inventor of the modern "ding-dong" doorbell, and together an influential couple in the arts of Cincinnati.

The long, narrow wing of brick that extends north from the auditorium is a Cobb original and houses the administrative offices of the college as well as some new classrooms. Along its length are four illumined pyramids that—reflecting Cobb's partnership with architect I. M. Pei—are reminiscent of the pyramidal entrance that Pei created for the Louvre, which so outraged Parisians more than a decade ago. Cobb's inclusion of the form has had no such effect on the faculty of the CCM and serves to break up what would otherwise be an excruciatingly monotonous low-slung roofline. Inside, the pyramids suffuse an open bi-level corridor with light. At the far end of the complex, tucked down a slope toward the athletic fields, is a new recital hall used for chamber orchestras and other small productions. The atrium features a large off-center glass overlook, which encompasses a view of most of the northeastern region of the campus, including Nippert Stadium, the central utilities power plant tower, and Michael Graves' magisterial Engineering Research Center. The siting of the new addition and this recital hall, however, creates tension with the master plan; one of the main directives of the plan was that all new development serve to connect the campus, which, it was held, had become fractured into fiefdoms. Part of the reason for the CCM Village, however, was to create a sense of identity and "place apart" for the students and faculty there, and the erection of this wing necessarily drives a wedge between the new CCM Village and the old academic ridge and new Main Street project.

TOP: *Mary Emery Hall (Mark Lyons)*
BOTTOM: *Corbett Pavilion scenery shop*

TOP: *Dieterle Center*
BOTTOM: *Dieterle Center*

Memorial Hall

In order to deal with this architectural conundrum, Cobb created a network of stairs and terraces that reaches around the northern facade, beneath and out of view of the glass wall of the recital hall, and up onto its roof. Here it bends back to another staircase, now descending, onto the plaza. At the rear of the building Cobb opened up the elevated plaza so that when the two new buildings across the street (almost two stories below) are finished, a skyway bridge can be built between all three. When completed this will create a major connector and thoroughfare between the eastern edge of campus (McMicken Commons) and the CCM Village, and Calhoun Street beyond.

The other tension Cobb had to reconcile was how to incorporate the two other buildings in the village, Memorial Hall and the Dieterle Center, both of which are more than seventy-five years old and of a distinctly traditional architectural style. The first of these, the Dieterle Center, was designed in 1910 by Garber & Woodward, architects of, among other buildings on campus, the Utilities Building on the north edge of Nippert Stadium (see Walk Two). Dieterle was originally built as the Schmidlapp Gymnasium, which included a natatorium in the basement. Cobb's renovation converted the entire structure into studios and performing space for the voice students. Many of the old touches of the building, including the magnificent windows overlooking campus and the vaulted atrium inside the southern doors, were retained and preserved. Cobb modernized the acoustics as best he could and tuned the recital hall specifically for vocal pitches.

Adjacent to Dieterle and slightly uphill is Memorial Hall. Originally designed in the Collegiate Gothic style by Cincinnati senior architect Harry

Memorial Hall gargoyles

Hake in 1924 as a residence hall, the building has now been converted into instrumental student studio space. The original design called for two interior garden courtyards "resplendent with grassy plots, silvery fountains and shady walks." The nucleus of the building—a central structure and tower—was erected first, with the other two wings intended to be built as enrollment rose; as the university evolved into a commuter campus, however, these were never completed. The facade of the building is festooned with parapets, abutments, and terracotta bas-reliefs depicting symbols of World War I, intended, as the building's appellation indicates, to memorialize the men from the university who gave their lives in the conflict. Panels around the main entrance include images of begoggled aviators and tanks mixed with traditional Gothic fare such as gargoyles. Like the literature of what came to be known as the Great War, the images belie an underlying darkness; the skeletons are frightening reminders that life in the trenches was nothing pretty—they bring to mind the stark realism of Randall Jarell's "Ball Turret Gunner," who "woke to black flak and the nightmare fighters." As part of the construction of CCM Village, Memorial Hall was gutted and redesigned to accommodate instrumental practice rooms and faculty offices. Cobb retained the important elements, including the magnificent fireplaces in many rooms and the vaulted ceilings. While the individual rooms were sheathed in four-ply wallboard to ensure absolute soundproofing, the doors were left alone so that the hallways remain awash in a cacophony of sound—a talisman of what goes on here.

In the center of the village, between each of these buildings, is a large automobile court, differentiated by a ring of pylons and spheres. Most

SOUTHEAST CAMPUS AND CCM VILLAGE

Light Mast (Mark Lyons)

visitors arriving in cars, however, simply drive into the parking garage beneath the structure, through an entrance well outside of the plaza. Thus, the gesture is more ceremonial, and in this way it feels European: an urban space meant for people. The CCM Village boasts the majority of the university's fledgling public art collection. In front of the James Werner Recital Hall sits *Figura Prima*, a bronze "hand tree" by Polish sculptor Magdalena Abakanowicz. In the back, affixed to the freestanding corner wall where bridges will soon connect CCM to the new Student Services building and Gwathmey Siegel's redesigned Tangeman Center, is a luminous glass tower by James Carpenter. Occupying the central wall of the new entrance to the Corbett Auditorium is a triptych by abstract painter Sam Gilliam, best known for his work at Ronald Reagan National Airport in Washington, D.C. The piece is constructed in birch plywood, piano hinges, and acrylic paint. A collage of musical symbols forms the skin.

Campus Green

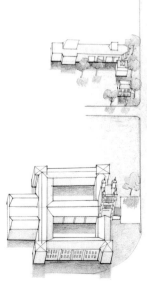

Clifton Avenue

McMicl
Commo

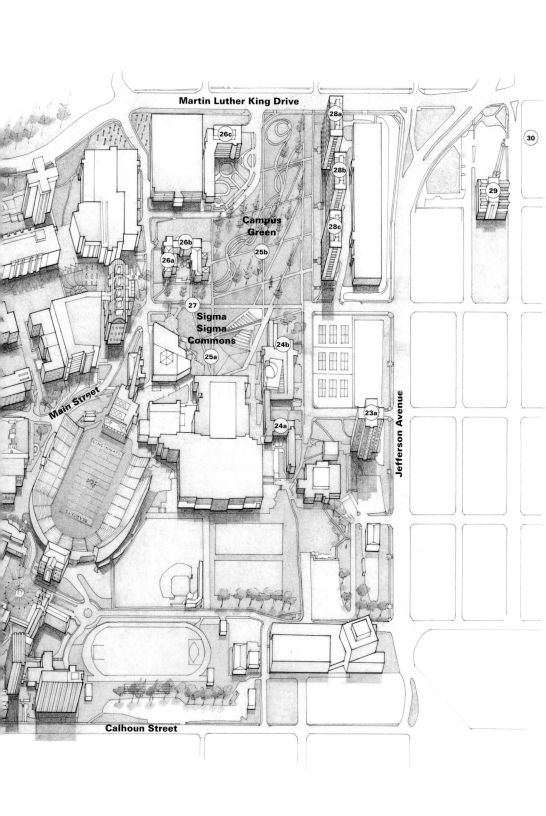

Martin Luther King Drive

26c

28a

30

29

28b

Campus
Green

26b

25b

28c

26a

27

Sigma
Sigma
Commons

24b

25a

Main Street

24a

23a

Jefferson Avenue

CINCINNATI

BEARCATS

Calhoun Street

The Residential Campus

Behind Baldwin Quad and the academic ridge, the campus of UC opens up into a large expanse, punctuated at the horizon by three oversized dormitories that look a lot like low-income housing projects. For decades the central feature of this part of campus was the sea of cars that basically extended from the edge of Campus Drive to these dorms. Functionally, the place was a disaster: hot as anything in the summer, filled with exhaust fumes and glaring sunlight. It was also depressing symbolically. Here was the heart of campus, and it was filled with Volkswagens and Chevys.

In the late 1980s the university commissioned landscape architect George Hargreaves to study possible alternatives to the parking lot. His proposal, developed with the help of his students at Harvard's Graduate School of Design, was to turn the area into a "campus green" that would become the central gathering place on campus. The idea lingered for years, eventually becoming codified in the master plan Hargreaves prepared, and finally designed and built in 2000. Today, the Campus Green is a locus of activity and one of the most important places on campus for the kind of learning that takes place outside of the classroom. Students can gather in the shady groves to study or debate, or in the amphitheater of nearby Sigma Sigma Commons; or they stroll through the mini-arboretum that lines a network of meandering paths; or they can surmount the eye-catching landforms at either end that make the landscape recognizable. However the space is used—and Hargreaves, for one, hopes that remains unpredictable—surely the Campus Green has come to signify a new emphasis on livability on campus.

The Green also signifies something that is fairly unusual on American campuses: a dedication on the part of the university's design committee to develop highly artful landscape spaces that exist on the same level as the campus's signature architecture. While it is probably remiss to call this a signature landscape architecture program—simply because no other signature landscape architect has been commissioned by the university besides Hargreaves—we do find at UC an uncommonly ambitious attitude toward landscape. At most academic institutions landscape is either relegated to traditionalism—the academic green dotted with mature trees of most Eastern schools—or dismissed altogether and turned over to horticulturists or plantsmen who, though well-intentioned, have little artistic sensibility. Hargreaves, however, and his partner Mary Margaret Jones, are very much artists who bring a sculptural and (they like to say) poetic sensibility to their work. The firm, Hargreaves Associates, cut its teeth at UC in the early 1990s, and since then has gone on to do several major commissions worldwide, including the design of all the open space at the Olympic Games 2000 in Sydney.

Like anything that breaks from the mold, Campus Green and Sigma Sigma Commons have been criticized, largely by people unfamiliar with avant-garde landscape design. Granted, there have been problems with functional aspects of the design, such as drainage and the ease with which the steeply sloped landforms or the oddly carved amphitheater can be mowed; but such difficulties are quite normal in experimental design. What matters, instead, is the spirit with which these spaces have been conceived and developed—a spirit that seeks not only to refine the mundane campus of UC but also to challenge the conservatism of campus design universally.

23. Daniels Hall and Sander Dining Hall

Daniels Hall *Bakie, Cates & Roth, 1967*
Sander Dining Hall *Woodie Garber, 1971*

Many people at the University of Cincinnati these days point to a June morning in 1991 as the turning point when the university finally decided to stop building bad architecture and commit to good architecture. On this day several thousand people turned out to watch the twenty-seven-story Sander Hall, a towering residence hall that, when constructed in 1971, was the tallest dorm in the state, implode and crumble to dust. What's left of Sander Hall today is architect Woodie Garber's companion piece, Sander Dining Hall, which

Daniels Hall

Sander Dining Hall

managed to escape unscathed—at least for now. Sander Hall, like the dining hall, was a Corbusier-inspired steel skyscraper with a curtain wall of glass and large concrete support pylons at each end. The dormitory, which housed over 1,300 students, was despised from the beginning. But the main reason it was torn down was because of fire hazards and poor emergency evacuation plans. The dining hall that remains is in poor shape, partly from neglect and partly from bad original design, which put the air vents next to the entrance and rimmed the entire building in an overhang of white rock gravel stuck in concrete. Across the parking lot from Sander Dining Hall sits another remnant from the skyscraper period, Daniels Hall, which is also a dormitory. The building is a Greek cross in plan. While certainly isolated and forbidding, Daniels Hall isn't as badly laid out as Sander, and thus has escaped the wrecking ball. It too features stone cladding around its roofline, something that must have been trend at one time.

24. Dabney Hall and French Hall

Dabney Hall *Potter, Tyler, Martin & Roth, 1960*
French Hall

> *Potter Tyler & Martin, James E. Allen, 1953;*
> *NBBJ and Wilson & Associates, addition, 1996*

Dabney Hall and French Hall were built seven years apart, to house students. The former, designed by Cincinnati architecture firm of Potter, Tyler, Martin & Roth, hovers on columns as a single, zigzagging, rectangular form in the International Style popular in the early 1960s. The detailing, however, is quite expressive. The tiled columns and striated limestone are two features that are very much coming back into vogue with postmodernists, and the massing of the building seems quite appropriate to its siting. Perhaps the best quality of the building is the way it forms space in the landscape and creates an intimate urban plaza between itself and the Armory. Dabney Hall feeds into French Hall, named after a benefactor of the university and designed by James Allen in association with Potter, Tyler & Martin in 1953. Like Dabney (or, rather, vice versa) it follows a zigzagging or chevron pattern.

These two humble brick boxes, reaching an unassuming five stories, were used as dormitories for many years until the need for classroom space at the University College became too great. The University College as well as the College of Evening and Continuing Education are both schools that serve the local community and have, in some manner, a lower profile than other colleges, such as the CCM or College of Engineering (both of which have new

Dabney Hall

TOP: *French Hall with Ampitheatre and Sigma Sigma*
BOTTOM: *French Hall, west roof*

French Hall

"signature" buildings). Despite this, the university hired local architectural firms of NBBJ and Wilson & Associates to design an addition to French Hall that in many ways is equal to the signature architecture projects elsewhere on campus. The new addition completely transfigures the existing architecture, essentially making it anew, by creating a semicircular "half donut" that rises in a courtyard of the old building to nearly double its height, consuming the previous building's mass and asserting one that is far more muscular and forward looking. Both firms, well versed in office building design, chose a silvery almost Richard Meier-like whiteness for the facade. From the outside, the most notable feature of the new design is the 7.5-degree slant of the building, which conforms to one of the "force fields" on campus created by the alignment of the Baldwin Quad at the top of the hill and other buildings that broke from the grid scheme earlier in the century. Like the Edwards Center design by David Childs (see Walk Four), the architecture emphasizes this slant and provides a kind of chorus to the circulation patterns created by Sigma Sigma Commons at its doorstep. Aesthetically the building makes its biggest statement within, especially where the banal brick edge of the old building is retained and framed by the sleek new architecture, creating a dialogue between two entirely different sensibilities—aesthetic bookends, of sorts, that describe the architectural trajectory of the campus in the last fifty years. Large skylights allow sunlight to reach the old windows and enliven what has now become the heart of the building. The orientation of the new addition and its nod to the master plan is best observed where the steps where they descend and meet with the sidewalk that paralleled the original French Hall.

25. Sigma Sigma Commons and Campus Green

Sigma Sigma Commons *Hargreaves Associates, 1998*
Campus Green *Hargreaves Associates, 2000*
Light Tower *Machado and Silvetti, 1998*

In 1989 landscape architect George Hargreaves was hired by the University of Cincinnati to help it develop a master plan (see the Introduction). This document, or perhaps more correctly the process that produced this document, is pretty much the driving force behind all that you see on campus today—and the subsequent rise of UC as one of the world's premier destinations for cutting-edge architecture. One of Hargreaves' key conclusions in the plan was that there were a series of different orientations—or what he called "force fields"—at work on campus, as a result of past planning strategies. Rather than try to favor one over another, he recommended that all be taken into consideration when siting new buildings and designing new open spaces. By embracing this palimpsest history Hargreaves was committing the university to a program of complex architecture, in which no building would ever be a simple rectangle sitting in an orthogonal grid. Sigma Sigma Commons allows one of the better perspectives on this strategy, laying it out in a way in very graphic terms.

The Commons was designed by Hargreaves and constructed in 1998 as the first part of a large open space plan for the heart of the West Campus. The site contains a change in topography as the small hillock on which the bookstore and fieldhouse rest slope down to what once was an expansive parking lot that stretched all the way to Martin Luther King Drive.

Sigma Sigma Commons

The site was also at the confluence of two of the force fields on campus. One was an orthogonal grid established by the academic ridge at the beginning of the campus's history and carried forth by the placement of French Hall, Dabney Hall, and the Armory Fieldhouse in this area. The second field was established by Nippert Stadium's off-axis kilter and its influence on the bookstore, Campus Drive, and general flow of traffic coming from the East Campus to the West Campus. In particular, this second force field in fact echoed the natural topography of the land, which slopes off the ridge in line with the stadium. At one time a small stream and marshy bottoms lay in this depression, but they have long since been filled in and diverted by underground sewers. Nonetheless, in order to deal with these force fields and the slope of the site, Hargreaves developed a scheme of wedges that descend from the bookstore and reflect the confluence of two orienting lines on campus. Working more as a sculptor than a technician, Hargreaves designed several large landforms, which, in effect, hide the ugly Fieldhouse from view and create grassy vistas from which to view the newly constructed Campus Green. There is also an amphitheater here, designed as slabs of granite set into grass and used primarily for impromptu hanging out by the students. At the ground level, where we find the heaviest traffic moving through campus, Hargreaves cut a swath of angled walkways, derived from the force fields, which point up their interplay at this crucial intersection. At the same time, the design privileges certain views over others. For instance, the straight perpendicular line that connects University Avenue with Michael Graves' Engineering Research Center is made wide and almost ceremonial—in part because this is a major thoroughfare, but also because the landscape architect recognized that Graves' building was rapidly becoming an icon on campus.

A donation by the venerable fraternity that is unique to UC enabled the construction of the Sigma Sigma Commons. Granite retaining slabs feature various members' names carved on them, and a memorial light tower stands watch over the northern edge of the space. The tower was designed by the Boston team of Rudolfo Machado and Jorge Silvetti, both originally from Argentina, who have established a respected practice in urban design. Both teach at Harvard and are perhaps best known for their work with the landscape architect Laurie Olin on Wagner Park in New York City. The Light Tower features a cast-in-place concrete base with letters 'U' and 'C' on alternating faces, and the upper portions are inscribed with the arcana of the fraternity, including the sign of the hammer and the Greek letter *sigma*. The culmination of the tower is the figurative flame at the top, constructed in perforated steel, which rotates and glows various colors.

In 2000 the university finally took down the orange construction fencing along the northern edge of Sigma Sigma Commons and opened the new Campus Green, an extensive open space that replaced an old surface

FOUNDING MEMBERS OF
SIGMA SIGMA

CHARLES W. ALLEN · WALTER KUMMERLE
ANDREW DIENINGER
SMITH HOENINGHOUS · ROBERT HUMBRECHT
KARL JONES · JAMES JOHNSON
RUSSELL MASON

FOUNDED OCTOBER 12, 1898

parking lot. The Green has actually been "on the boards" since the beginning of the master planning process in the late 1980s. It was at this time that Hargreaves was asked to submit a proposal for turning the parking lot into a green. He used the problem as an assignment in a studio he was teaching at Harvard, and from the students' initial explorations he further elaborated the design—over almost a decade—into what we see today. The central spine of the green is a "braid" of interweaving walkways, which are derived from the form of an old stream that once ran through this area. Between the walks are paramecium-shaped landforms planted with hornbeams and other hearty trees. At the culmination of the space the braid unites into a single walk that circles and almost ascends a large conical hill, sculpted to create a kind of ziggurat or lookout over the campus and planted with creeping vines. At the base are a series of curved water walls, built in granite and planted with cypress, a water loving tree. Along the eastern edge of the space are wedge-shaped groves (connecting visually with the wedge theme established in Sigma Sigma Commons) elevated above the walkways. The landscape's groundplane material is decomposed granite, sandstone in color to harmonize with the visual markers at the entrance of the university and Michael Graves' Engineering Research Center, and planted with magnolias, which, as they mature, should provide dense shade and vibrant blossoms. In the upland section of the green there are several small lawns, something desperately needed on campus for light recreation like Frisbee, etc.

In the master plan, the Campus Green is the first step towards creating a string of landscape spaces (the so-called "string of pearls") that will eventually connect the East and West Campuses. The Main Street project will complete that process on the West Campus, and then planners and landscape architects will start looking for ways to cross the hazardous intersection at the top of the hill.

26. Faculty and Alumni Center and Lindner Hall

Faculty Center *Cellarius & Hilmer, 1969*
Myers Alumni Center *Glaser, Myers & Associates, 1988*
Lindner Hall *Gartner, Burdick, Bauer-Nilson Architects, 1986*

The benefactor of the Faculty Center, Murray Seasongood, a founder of the Republican Charter Party, was a lover of Frank Lloyd Wright, which explains the low-slung roofline, sensitivity to the surroundings, and general look of the building that honors him. The Myers Alumni Center was built almost twenty years later, but shows an appreciation for the original Faculty Center

OPPOSITE: *Light Tower*

Faculty Center

and seems to approximate it quite well. The architects of the older building were Cellarius and Hilmer, a local architecture firm known for its traditionalism. Cellarius, in particular, was adept at Colonial Revival buildings, so it is notable that this structure is far outside his usual idiom. In terms of a Wright knockoff it is quite good. The roofline is most striking, with shifting planes reducing the visual mass of the building and allowing it to suffuse with the landscape. Between the two buildings, which are now conjoined, lies a pleasant little courtyard planted with four symmetrically arranged copper beech trees; though it's a comfortable space the rigid formality of the landscape, which Wright would have detested, exposes the true authorship. The later building was designed by Glaser, Myers & Associates, a Cincinnati firm known for, among other things, the renovation of the downtown art museum and several other buildings on campus.

Lindner Hall, designed by the Ohio office-building firm of GBBN, Inc., is a solid rectangular mass of building that sits in a slight depression along the edge of Campus Green. The architecture itself is rather uneventful—save for the simple, abstract geometrical decorations on the eastern side and the way the building's form carves out a pleasant courtyard in front. Here we find concrete sculptural seating and light-filtering honey locust trees.

27. Entrance Gateway *George Hargreaves, 1995*

Hargreaves' comprehensive work on the campus included the design of a gateway language, which is employed at the key entrances of the campus. A polygonal-shaped grid of pylons stands in a rolling field of grass. The pinnacle of the pylons forms a plane, against which the topography of the ground plane rises or falls, giving a sense of kineticism and drawing visual connections to Stonehenge, Easter Island, and cemetery architecture. In Hargreaves' hands the idea is to make one aware less of the pylons—attractively composed of a rare vein-riddled Briar Hill sandstone and bands of weathered copper—than of the movement of the landscape, a subtle gesture that nonetheless resonates with the most landscape-illiterate visitor. Hargreaves' use of the sandstone, a departure from the red brick and white Indiana limestone vocabulary of the traditional campus architecture, has set a precedent on campus and can be seen in Michael Graves' Engineering Research Building and the new Kingsgate complex on East Campus. Architect Mauricio Luzuriaga, who works in the office of the university architect and oversees many of the architectural projects on campus, says that "it's getting to the point where we've thought about buying the mine that produces it [Briar Hill sandstone]. It's becoming difficult to find exactly the right veins." This gateway is one of several you will see at key entrance points on the campus.

28. The Three Sisters

Morgens Hall *F.W. Pressler & Associates, 1964*
Scioto Hall *F.W. Pressler & Associates, 1964*
Sawyer Hall *F.W. Pressler & Associates, 1964*

Sitting in a jagged line along the ridge that separates the East and West Campuses are the "three sisters" residence halls: Morgens, Scioto, and Sawyer. The small apartments within are used by graduate students. The architecture falls broadly into the International Style, although the decorative elements point to a more stylized or Mannerist interpretation of that normally sleek and unadorned approach. Although in poor shape, the building features diverse and unconventional materials—such as the exterior cladding of perforated metal, tiled pylons, and corrugated metal—very much in vogue these days. Nevertheless, the buildings are rightly despised for their massive scale and for the way they form a barrier between the two halves of campus at a time when most people want to build bridges. One proposal for repair is to strip off the exterior down to the structural frame (which is in good shape), cut the buildings in half to reduce their height, and restore the interiors and exteriors as part of a larger residential structure to be erected atop of the

Morgens, Scioto, and Sawyer Halls, with Light Tower

parking structure along Jefferson Avenue. This is just a dreamy idea, of course, and one that would have to fit into the overall master plan scheme and ambitious building schedule already in process. But we can find dreams like this all over campus, many of which have been undertaken.

29. Central Utility Plant *Cambridge Seven in association with URS, 1992*

In the late 1980s the university embarked on a plan to build a second generator plant outside of the heart of campus, in order to eventually dismantle the loud, groaning plant adjacent to Nippert Stadium (see Walk Two). The plan, however, immediately became contentious with residents of Corryville, as the neighborhood across Vine Street is called. The residents feared the university would built a similar nuisance, in effect shipping its power problem into their backyard in order to clean up its own yard. To find a solution the university called in the Boston architectural firm of Cambridge Seven. According to university architect Ron Kull, Cambridge Seven's work on the attractive and successful light-rail stations around Boston had been exercised with utmost sensitivity to community concerns. The firm, in particular its managing director Charles Redmon, was known for being able to work with community groups and nonarchitects well, without letting the final design of buildings drift into banality or devolve into the "architecture of the lowest common denominator."

OPPOSITE: *Central Utility Plant*

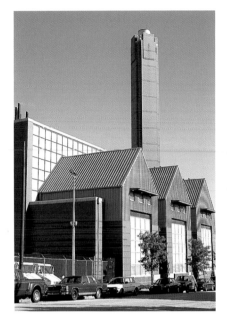 

Central Utility Plant

The utility plant, because of its engineering needs, is actually a large rectangular structure that would have seemed ungainly on a residential street, so the architects designed a series of three house-shaped bays with pitched rooflines and colorful corrugated material. The scale and shape of the bays conform to the general look of the neighborhood—on first glance one might miss that they hide a power plant at all. The single stack was then clad in deep red brick and twisted off center, so that from the predominate viewing points it is seen corner-on rather than side on, a trick that reduces its visual mass. The brick ties into the old church on the corner. The glass block windows on Vine Street are illuminated at night, giving light to a dark street and helping to cut down on crime.

At the same time that these touches are used to integrate the building into its context and conceal the power plant functioning inside, Cambridge Seven also gave the utility plant artistic touches that draw attention to the building and, theoretically at least, cultivate some bonds of affection with it. The blue color of the bays is warm and striking; the small red lights on each facade create a technological presence at night. Much of the detailing at street level is a confection of fiberglass that serves no purpose other than to lift the building from the mundane and make it more special than a typical power plant. Sitting as it does on the crest of a hill and at the important intersection of the two halves of the university campus—and also at the point where the campus greets its neighbors—the building functions ultimately as a beacon or gateway that welcomes, invites, and hopefully pleases most visitors—providing they don't pass it by.

Corryville Library

The little neighborhood of Corryville, located across Vine Street from the East Campus, features several attractive old houses in the Queen Anne and Tudor styles. Some are in poor shape, but several have been restored. At No. 2823 Eden Avenue is a new community recreation center designed by Brenda and Michael Scheer, UC professors of planning and architecture, respectively. The building, obviously built on a low budget, is nonetheless quite wonderful and sensitively designed. The exterior is red brick (in keeping with the local context) with galvanized metal trim around the windows, an overt nod to the Vontz Center nearby (see Walk Six). Glass block in the bays between the windows lets light into the structure while giving the exterior facade variety and rhythm. On the corner the architecture culminates in a semicircular window, which allows views through to the large ballet studio inside. A Brutalist treatment of exposed concrete, with the construction marks still visible, adds contrast to the use of brick and metal. Inside, the structure is divided into large gyms on one side, smaller exercise rooms on the other, and a central transept between with elevated skylights that bathe what might otherwise be a cavernous place in light.

Corryville Recreation Center

East Campus Medical Complex

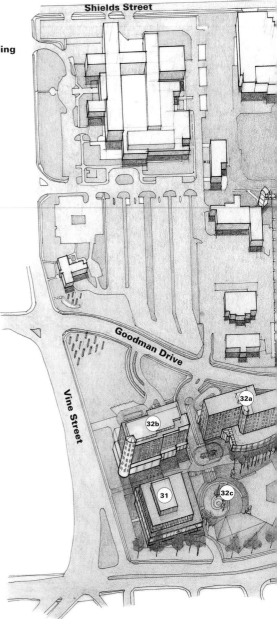

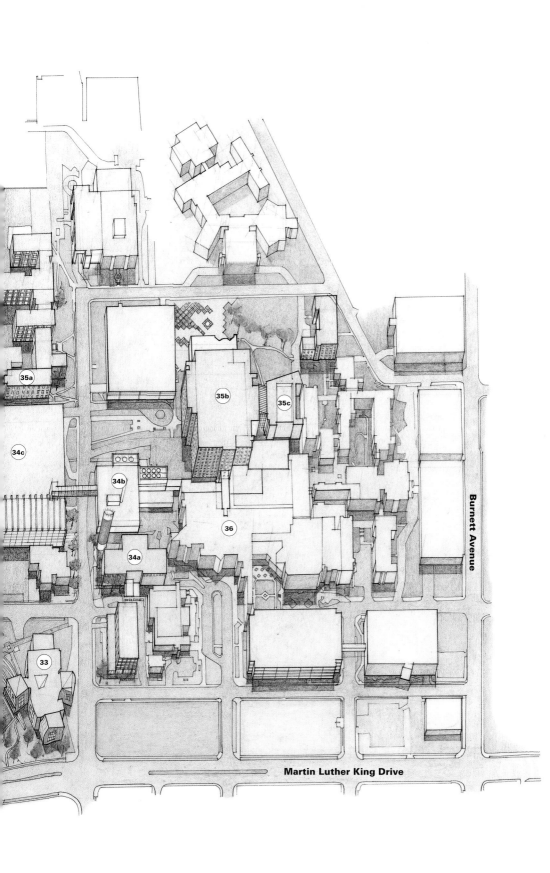

The campus of the University of Cincinnati is actually two campuses, with the east half located over the hill and beyond the busy intersection of Vine Street and Martin Luther King Drive. Traveling between the two can be a nightmarish dodge through traffic, not to mention quite a bit of a hike. It's not uncommon to see students and faculty driving a car simply to travel from an office on one campus to a classroom on another.

The College of Medicine, which dominates the East Campus, was originally founded in 1819 at the Medical College of Ohio by Daniel Drake, an energetic Cincinnati educational booster considered one of the fathers of the university. However, it was almost a hundred years before the college would actually become a part of the university and move to its present hilltop abode. Today, the College of Medicine is one of the university's anchor institutions. In the 1990s, the hospital used by the college was split off as a private hospital for various legal and economic reasons—although due to its strong ties to the college its buildings are mentioned here. However, the future of the College is one without a hospital, and therefore the architectural focus of the campus is currently changing away from large public buildings and towards more specialized research facilities. The most obvious example of this is the Vontz Center for Molecular Studies, designed by Frank Gehry and opened for business in 1999. This is a state-of-the-art research facility, boasting not only some of the most technologically advanced laboratory space in the country but also some of the most striking architecture anywhere. Gehry's work at the Vontz, though much smaller and more restrained than his masterwork at Bilbao, Spain, stands as a seminal project in his oeuvre. We see here the mature Gehry, with sculptural forms still pushing envelopes and introducing new ideas, but with less of the brash, unworkable attributes of his earlier buildings.

The Vontz was placed at a key entry into the East Campus—at the place through which most automobile visitors pass—in order to make a statement about where the university's East Campus is headed. Although divided from the West Campus geographically and culturally, the East Campus is very much a part of the master planning effort. The Vontz actually sits in a precinct of new buildings, including the Kingsgate Conference Center and University Commons, with a striking garden by landscape architect George Hargreaves. Further into the campus there is new work occurring on the Medical Sciences Buildings, which is the core of the college. At the same time, a redesign of Eden Avenue promises to connect to a pedestrian pathway system that will facilitate movement from one campus to the other. The missing link in this plan is the unsolved traverse over the hill and intersection, which conspire to act as a virtual roadblock between the campuses. In his master plan, Hargreaves has proposed a pedestrian bridge that would arch gracefully from the walkway in front of the Kingsgate Center over the edge of the Campus Green. Such an object could be processed through the signature architecture program and, owing to its visibility, would further heighten UC's stature as a destination for architecture. But all of this is presently just an idea that has to survive a gauntlet of state and municipal planners who have jurisdiction of these streets.

Generally speaking a walk through the East Campus is an adventure through the most polyglot part of the university, where, as a university architect put it, we find "a mass of buildings with few corresponding to the one next to it." Despite the few really bad pieces of architecture there are some surprising gems, such as the Cardiovascular Research Center and the Eden Avenue Garage, as well, of course, as the masterpiece of Gehry's Vontz.

31. Procter Hall *Woodie Garber, 1968*

Architect Woodie Garber's father, Frederick, designed several of the old Georgian buildings that line Clifton Avenue in the historic core of the campus, including Teachers College and Baldwin Hall. Woodie, in contrast, emphatically rejected the historicist styles of his father and instead embraced modernism, which from the beginning had advocated a rejection of past styles. Woodie Garber's own architecture, however, lacked the simplicity of early modernism; instead of the severe, naked geometries of

Procter Hall

TOP: *University Hall*
BOTTOM: *Kingsgate Conference Center*

Gropius, Mies or Corbusier, Garber adorned his buildings with almost rococo confections. Procter Hall, Garber's monumental gateway to the East Campus, is ringed by a skirt of white-gravel cast into concrete. Between a band at the top and one in the middle lies the habitable space of the building, vertically constructed with steel girders and narrow windows protected by sun louvers. Inside, students complain about the impracticality of the design, most notably that it is difficult to move between floors. Despite this, the interior features a large circular staircase built in steel with oak treads. But by far the biggest failing has been a lack of maintenance, in part because it is expensive or impossible to fix things. Much of the white gravel has fallen off, leaving behind a *concrete brute* facing pocked with holes. The front of the building, facing Vine Street, is missing its bridge entrance and looks naked and neglected. The building was named after William Cooper Procter, a benefactor and grandson of one of the founders of the Procter and Gamble Company. Procter currently houses the nursing school.

32. Kingsgate Conference Center, University Hall, and University Commons

Kingsgate Conference Center and University Hall *VOA, 1999*
University Commons *George Hargreaves, 1999*

The Kingsgate complex is the only new architecture on campus since the 1989 master plan that was commissioned as the result of an actual competition— meaning that instead of just interviewing architects and trying to match buildings to designers according to specialty or proclivity, specific proposals with numbers were submitted for review. However, unlike typical design competitions where architects submit proposals simply for the construction of the building and are judged on the merit of their design (and oftentimes budget), the Kingsgate complex was a comprehensive competition; architects were required to team up with developers and financiers and create an entire package for the complex. In this case that also meant finding a tenant who would pay for one half of the complex and thus finance the construction of the other half. Chicago architects VOA teamed up with Marriott and won the job; half of the complex is given over to the developer's conference center and hotel.

VOA used the same Briar Hill sandstone in its design as campus master planner and landscape architect George Hargreaves employed in the entrance pylons that mark several key gateways around campus. The buildings are situated on a line tracking downhill from Vine Street—forming an edge to the lower landscape designed by Hargreaves. One of the hopes of the conference center was that it would raise the stature of the university by bringing more national groups onto the campus, making them aware of UC's premiere programs, such as those in the sciences, music, engineering, and architecture. It was also envisioned that UC's colleges might employ the multi-media component of the conference center for distance learning and other cutting-edge pedagogical pursuits. The design of the structures is rather plain, if strong and handsome. The stone facing is expressed in large blocks and capped with various cupolas and terraces. Perhaps the most important move of the architects, as concerns the overall development of campus and the master plan, was the design and construction of an open-air terrace off the conference center, hosting an outdoor restaurant. The terrace itself lies on an important axis that is part of the new circulation pattern of green spaces, the so-called string of pearls, which connects the East and West Campuses. The building bulges out at this point to pinch the walkway, creating an intimate, almost urban feeling, enhanced by the overlook to the garden below. Hargreaves designed the garden, called University Commons. It echoes the aesthetic of other spaces on campus, recalling the entry markers through the use of sandstone coloring and the Kingsgate Center in the decomposed granite groundcover and the conical ziggurat topped by a garden of columnar trees.

33. Vontz Center for Molecular Studies

Frank O. Gehry in association with Baxter Hodell Donnelly & Preston, 2000

Since the unveiling of his Guggenheim museum in Bilbao in 1997, Frank O. Gehry has quickly become America's, if not the world's, most celebrated architect. Gehry's architectural work (he also designs smaller art objects, such as furniture) is characterized by two main features. The first is a sense of sculptural form. The museum at Bilbao looks as if it were carved from clay, a challenging building form that looks almost cartoonish or Martian in appearance. The second feature of his work, which separates Gehry from his contemporaries in architecture today, is the use of unconventional mate-rials. In one of his most famous structures, his own office building in Santa Monica, Gehry used corrugated metal and a plethora of other "found" materials to create what to many looks like a junkyard building. Architec-turally, however, it made a statement that buildings could be transformed— not just aesthetically but in meaning as well—by attending to construction materials, so often an afterthought in design.

The Vontz Center for Molecular Studies was commissioned prior to Bilbao and completed after it, and in every way expresses these two charac-teristics of the Gehry style. The outward form of the building, an abstracted Greek cross of four cubes meeting in the middle, is absolutely sculptural. The sides bow outward, the rooftops bend forward; the entire structure seems animated and positively unstructured. And yet it is highly structured. Gehry created the Vontz using a cardboard model, which his office then

ABOVE AND OPPOSITE: *Vontz Center for Molecular Studies*

digitized by scanning it with laser and transferring the dimensional data to a three-dimensional computer program. It is this handmade-to-computer-made process that some critics have noted gives the architect's work a certain organic quality. There is something about a Gehry building, while fanciful and imaginative, that seems to come from nature, flowerlike. Certainly this idea is given weight at the Vontz Center by the use of brick—a novelty for the architect, whose signature use of burnished, corrugated, and colored metals rather than traditional stone or concrete or brick is well known. The University of Cincinnati was surprised by the choice and by the fact that this unconventional architect argued for it based on local tradition. Gehry's position may have stemmed from frustration. Up to his selection for the Vontz Center Gehry had been shortlisted for the DAAP project, the Engineering Research Building, and a residence on campus that had been canceled. In all cases he'd been passed over, despite the fact that he was one of the few competitors who had won architecture's top honor, the Pritzker Prize. The Vontz commission was a much anticipated blessing from the university, and Cincinnati, and in thanks Gehry chose to work in the local style—red brick, ubiquitous throughout the older parts of the city.

Gehry's initial impulse was to construct the building in laid brick, but very quickly a problem arose. How does one manage the curves with laid brick without having to fabricate a new shaped brick at each layer, as the building arches and swings in novel ways? The budget for such a scheme would have been outrageous, so Gehry suggested fabricating brick panels, which could then be hung, very much like curtain walls, from the internal

structure. Gehry specified a brick made in Utah that contained high levels of

pink; however, when it came time to fabricate the panels for the Vontz, the clay vein that the Utah brick maker was tapping turned out, deep inside the earth, to be much darker than expected. By mixing and matching bricks from different fabrication batches, Gehry achieved uniformity at a distance, though close up one can see wonderful variation, sort of like a pointillist painting. Although the building shimmers in the light of dusk with a pinkish brilliance, it is interesting to note that the architect would have had it more so.

The construction of the panels was a laborious undertaking. The manufacturer, because of the individuality of each panel and the fact that when they were all completed they had to fit together, required Gehry and the local architecture firm Baxter Hodell Donnelly Preston (BHDP) to provide three-dimensional data—x, y, and z coordinates—for every foot of the design. The panels were then hung. At the joinery the construction crews and BHDP intended to use a caulk that matched the mortar of the brick, so that from a distance the skin would appear as uninterrupted brick; however, when it proved difficult to find, Gehry advised them to forget it and use what they had—a dark gray caulk that reveals the component nature of the construction and accentuates the fact that these are individual panels and not real bricks. But the lines also created an additional architectural layer, a grid that overlays Gehry's design—so that we see the forms as if they were sketched on graph paper. It's yet another unexpected twist of complexity in a hyper-complex building. The edges of the forms, where panels meet at angles, were finished in galvanized steel. The trickiest parts of the building were the throats, which are barely perceptible from the outside. These are the curved connectors between the forms on the north and on the south of the building, and which curve in two directions at once—the formidable and feared compound curve in architecture.

Gehry hired Earl Walls to consult on the actual design of the laboratory, which had to represent the most cutting-edge design. Walls gained a reputation with his work on Louis Kahn's Salk Institute in La Jolla, California—a building hailed as the most beautiful and most functional lab in the world, two praises rarely combined in the same breath. One of the key decisions made by Walls was to fit the Vontz with interstitial floors between each laboratory floor, as he'd done at the Salk. In essence, while we see three floors inside the building, between each one there is a small floor—eight feet tall compared to the fifteen-foot height of the regular floor. This is used as a staging area when laboratories are reconfigured, thereby minimalizing disruption to the rest of the facility when one project ends and another begins. In a place like the Vontz Center, which is a multidisciplinary building inhabited by individual research teams fueled on a diet of grants that come and go, lab redesigns happen with frustrating frequency. "Labs are supposed to change twenty percent a year," explains Carl Monzel principal of BHDP, thereby

Vontz Center for Molecular Studies

implying that if they don't they're simply not keeping up with currents in the field. "That means that every five years you have a new building."

The lab design is very straightforward, with the three floors basically containing an interior block of heavy equipment (superfreezers, atom smashers, and the like) surrounded by a ring of homogenous lab space, which is then ringed by desk space at the windows. The interior architecture of walls and ceiling (including the interstitial space above) was pulled back from the exterior skin and windows so that at the edge of the lab the windows run the full length of the floor—flooding the space with light, intense at times. Interestingly, the inhabitants complain about too much sunlight, just as did the inhabitants of Kahn's Salk Lab. Unlike Kahn, however, Gehry hasn't resisted the impulse to fit his windows with blinds. The interior of the Vontz is finished in a very minimalist style, with Gehry's signature low-end materials. Lightly stained Douglas fir plywood is used throughout, with edges left untrimmed. In the 140-person auditorium, located just off the atrium, this technique reaches its pinnacle in the perforated plywood wall that surrounds the room. Gehry specified the holes to be larger than a quarter, magically transforming the mundane material into something majestic. In the atrium one finds more Gehry woodwork in a series of cases that houses a collection of memorabilia of the later Albert Sabin, a famous UC scientist who developed the oral polio vaccine. The two north and south wings house offices, each of which is of a different dimension, and many of which, on the first floor at least, feature slanting windows, and on the third floor a sloping roof. The most magical and exciting places within the building are at the interstices between forms. Here Gehry left slight cracks or open spaces, enclosed by glass. One purpose of this is simply to let natural light filter into the building. It also has the effect of emphasizing the forms from within so that in standing at one of these interstices you perceive one form falling away to one side and another in another direction.

Gehry asserts that he loves scientists for their forward-thinking minds. In light of this, the building was thought to be a perfect match between client (the researchers who were going to live there) and architect. The form is the architectural equivalent of molecular science—cutting edge, progressive, creative, and open to new ideas. The building was funded in large part by Alfred Vontz, an alumnus businessman who owns the Heidelberg Distribution Company. Unfortunately, because of the sensitive nature of the research that goes on in the Vontz, public access is limited normally to the atrium and the small display on Sabin.

Walking around the building we find a grand staircase descending from the western face and opening out onto the garden. Here, at the foot of the building, rests sculptor Terry Allen's "Belief," an oversized bronze leaf that, in its realism, contrasts starkly with the fantastic architecture.

34. French East, Power Plant, and
Eden Avenue Garage

French East *Ellerbe Associates and Potter, Tyler, Martin & Roth, 1970*
East Campus Power Plant

> *Samuel Hannaford and Sons, 1914; Shepley & Richardson, addition, 1963;*
> *William Sammons, addition, 1989*

Eden Avenue Garage *Kral Zepf Freitag, 1988*

Crossing Eden Avenue from the Vontz Center we begin to enter the precincts of the College of Medicine. Immediately kitty corner from the Vontz is a monolithic box known as French East, which today houses classrooms for the medical college and computer labs. The building was originally part of the Shriners' Burn Institute and then turned over to the college when that institution moved to a new location. The cornice is ringed by a crown of windows with concrete trim in a heavy almost Brutalist style. Over the entrance is an odd stylistic feature: a massive block of granite, which gives the building a peculiarly haphazard balance and breaks the monotony of the composition. Although a fairly minimal building, it is also thankfully pure, especially with the line of trees planted against the plain concrete walls.

Next door to French East, farther down Eden Avenue, is another old power plant that has been added onto several times. The original structure was designed by Samuel Hannaford and Sons in 1914. They were the architects for the original McMicken Hall and Old St. George, which still stands

French East

LEFT: *Eden Avenue Garage*
RIGHT: *East Campus Power Plant*

on Calhoun Street. Much of the original power plant is now obscured by successive additions and redesigns, including especially the neon orange tower that looks like it walked off the set of Sesame Street or out of a Kindergarten classroom.

Across the street from the power plant is the Eden Avenue garage, which was added onto by local architectural firm Kral Zepf Freitag (KZF) in 1998. The addition is really quite lovely, with the exoskeleton exposed and cylinders of glass placed at the ends. The red brick hints make intelligent connections to the rest of campus, while the bridge across Eden Avenue, clad in glass, perforated metal, and exposed concrete, is a wonderful amalgam of old and new. The garage is a grand example of a design that appreciates the aesthetics of industrialism and doesn't shy from expressing the utilitarianism of functionality—a design that at the same time gives expression to form. It's more than just a parking garage, and yet doesn't try to be something it's not. At ground level, Eden Avenue is getting a facelift by landscape architect George Hargreaves, with plans for canopied walkways separated by his signature mounded earth forms and botanically rich plantings. This new greenway will connect with the walkway along the front (south side) of the Kingsgate Center to create the major circulation thoroughfare between the two halves of the campus.

35. Wherry Hall, Medical Sciences Building, and Cardiovascular Research Center

Wherry Hall *Kruckmeyer and Strong, 1959*
Medical Sciences Building *Ellerbe Associates, 1973*
Cardiovascular Research Center *Baxter Hodell Donnelly Preston, 1999*

Wherry Hall, which houses the pharmaceutical science department at the College of Medicine, was designed in 1959 by Cincinnati firm Kruckmeyer and Strong. The form is that of a Greek Temple, placed on site geometrically to develop a grid structure for the placement of future buildings on the eastern campus.

Across the street from Wherry Hall is the decidedly drab Medical Sciences Building, designed by the St. Paul, Minnesota-based firm Ellerbe Associates in 1973. It is scheduled for a major redesign. The dramatic expansion, dubbed the Center for Allied Research and Education and nicknamed CARE, will involve razing the existing decrepit garage, which is practically falling down on its own accord, and wrapping the existing Medical Sciences Building with a new structure. The university has hired Studios Architecture, a California firm that made a name for itself in the 1990s with a series of commissions for Silicon Valley high-tech office buildings, to do the work. Studios principle-in-charge will be Eric Suberkrop, a graduate of UC.

The interior of the existing Medical Sciences Building is like a morgue and unfortunately has to be traversed in order to reach the new Cardiovascular Research Center behind. Designed by Cincinnati architects

Medical Sciences Building

Baxter Hodell Donnelly Preston, it is as airy, comfortable, and grand as the adjoining Medical Sciences Building is horrendously depressing. This building illustrates one of the problems with the university's signature architect program—by putting so much emphasis on out-of-town, internationally recognized architects, local firms that do exceptional work can get overlooked. The main space of the Cardiovascular Research Center (CRC) is a tall, open atrium crisscrossed by walkway bridges that feed elevator silos. The proportion, scaling, and massing of the components are all sensitively executed, creating a breathtaking effect. The offices along the eastern wall of the space, all windowed, give one the sense of being in a massive museum and looking in on the researchers within. Hanging in the middle of the space is a mobile constructed by Tim Prentice, an architect who made the jump to sculpture. It is titled "Art Beat." Unfortunately the CRC is wedged into an impossibly tight spot, and it is nearly impossible to view it from outside. From the small courtyard on the north side, accessed through a set of glass doors, you can view a slight sliver of the structure and the wedge-shaped corner that seems derived from Peter Eisenman's Aronoff Center for Design across campus. In order to discover this little architectural gem, enter the Medical Sciences Building on the ground floor, take the elevator one floor up, and press on toward the back of the building, looking for signs to the CRC.

36. University Hospital

Samuel Hannaford & Sons, 1914–1955; Shepley & Richardson, addition, 1969

In the mid-1990s the university, following a trend nationwide, privatized the hospital. Because the university is a public institution and prohibited from engaging in private enterprise, it then disassociated itself legally from the hospital. Culturally and architecturally, however, the hospital remains very much a part of university life. It is still a teaching hospital used by medical professors in the adjacent College of Medical Sciences. And most importantly for our purposes, it was built as a university institution. The original hospital was designed by Samuel Hannaford and Sons, a Cincinnati architectural institution and responsible for several other buildings on campus, such as the original McMicken Hall and St. George Church. The old hospital consisted of a sequence of separate pavilions, all designed in dark brick in a plain Georgian style that was, nonetheless, quite handsome. In 1969, with the hospital then serving a large community and under pressure from the city to open its doors to indigents and poor patients, it undertook the construction of a new modern hospital, dubbed General Hospital. The architect for this expansion was the Boston firm Shepley & Richardson, an old American firm originally started by H.H. Richardson in the nineteenth

LEFT: *Deaconess Hospital*
RIGHT: *University Hospital entrance*

century. By 1969, however, the firm was practicing in a contemporary idiom that lacked much of its founder's originality. The outward form of General Hospital is a hodgepodge of polygonal shapes bulging from a square base. The only hint of Richardson himself lies in the small French-styled courtyard garden, where patients on good days sit and enjoy the air. Hidden behind this massive edifice are many of the old pavilions designed by Hannaford, which appear like haunted architectural vestiges. Most of them are still in use by various medical institutions not associated with the school. The hospital, although not officially part of the university, is used by the College of Medicine as a teaching institution.

OPPOSITE: *University Hospital complex*

Bibliography

Clubbe, John. *Cincinnati Observed*. Ohio State University Press, 1992.

"Development by Degrees: The Reinvention of the University of Cincinnati." *World Architecture* (September 1999).

Findsen, Owen. "Jayanta Chatterjee: Enquirer Profile." *Cincinnati Enquirer*, January 9, 1994.

Forgey, Benjamin. "Ivory Towers: University of Cincinnati's Clear View." *Washington Post*, October 5, 1996.

Giglierano, Geoffrey. *Bicentennial Guide to Greater Cincinnati*. Cincinnati Museum Center, 1989.

Giovannini, Joseph. "Peter Eisenman's Aronoff Center." *Architectural Record* (August 1996).

Gordon, Steve. "Samuel Hannaford." Unpublished paper presented to the Society of Architectural Historians Annual Conference, Pittsburgh, PA, 1985.

Grace, Kevin and Greg Hand. *The University of Cincinnati*. Montgomery, Alabama: Community Communications, 1995.

Higginbotham, Mickey. "Kaboom, Sander Hall Bites the Dust." *The Cincinnati Enquirer*. June 24, 1991.

Langsam, Walter. *Great Houses of the Queen City*. Cincinnati Historical Society, 1997.

McGrane, Reginald. *The University of Cincinnati: A Success Story in Urban Higher Education*. New York: Harper and Row Publishers, 1963.

Schoenbaum, David. "Building a New Conservatory the American Way." *New York Times*. June 4, 2000.

Stephens, Suzanne. "The American Campus." *Architectural Record*, February 2000.

Turner, Paul Venable. *Campus: An American Planning Tradition*. Cambridge, MA: The MIT Press, 1984.

Wiseman, Carter. *Twentieth Century American Architecture*. W.W. Norton & Co., 2000.

Acknowledgments

This book could not have been written without the tremendous support of the University of Cincinnati, especially Jay Chatterjee, Ron Kull, Dale McGirr—dean of the College of Design, Art, Architecture and Planning, university architect, and vice president of finance, respectively. They and the design review committee, along with the consulting architects both "signature" and local, have put the muscle behind the campus's transformation in the last decade. Also at UC, I must thank architect Mauricio Luzuriaga, who spent countless hours facilitating my research; archivist Kevin Grace, who gave me access to the archive crypts and helped filter reams of historical data; landscape architect Len Thomas, Sandra Harding in the university architect's office, and Walter E. Langsam, son of the former president of UC, whose knowledge of the history of Cincinnati architecture was invaluable. George Hargreaves provided much information about the master planning process. Jan Cigliano, my editor, was critical in getting it all together. Walter Smalling's smart photography made all the difference. None of this at all would be possible without the love and support of my wife, Lani Bevacqua.